P9-CQB-914

BY JULIA BAIRD

*Media Tarts: How the Australian Press
Frames Female Politicians*

Victoria: The Queen

Phosphorescence

Phosphorescence

Phosphorescence

A Memoir of Finding Joy
When Your World Goes Dark

JULIA BAIRD

Random House
New York

Copyright © 2020 by Julia Baird

All rights reserved.

Published in the United States by Random House, an imprint
and division of Penguin Random House LLC, New York.

RANDOM HOUSE and the HOUSE colophon are registered
trademarks of Penguin Random House LLC.

Originally published in Australia by Fourth Estate,
an imprint of HarperCollins Publishers, in 2020.

Some of the essays in this work or portions thereof appeared in
different form on the Australian Broadcasting Corporation's
website (abc.net.au) and in *The New York Times*,
Newsweek, and *The Sydney Morning Herald*.

Permission credits appear on page 289.

LIBRARY OF CONGRESS CATALOGING-IN-PUBLICATION DATA
Names: Baird, Julia (Julia Woodlands), author.
Title: Phosphorescence: a memoir of finding joy
when your world goes dark / Julia Baird.
Description: First edition. | New York: Random House, [2021] |
Includes bibliographical references.
Identifiers: LCCN 2020038625 (print) | LCCN 2020038626 (ebook) |
ISBN 9780593236918 (hardcover) | ISBN 9780593236925 (ebook)
Subjects: LCSH: Baird, Julia (Julia Woodlands)—Health. |
Ovaries—Cancer—Patients—United States—Biography. |
Philosophy of nature. | Hope. | Phosphorescence.
Classification: LCC RC280.O8 B325 2021 (print) |
LCC RC280.O8 (ebook) |
DDC 616.99/465—dc23
LC record available at https://lccn.loc.gov/2020038625
LC ebook record available at https://lccn.loc.gov/2020038626

Printed in Canada on acid-free paper

randomhousebooks.com

2 4 6 8 9 7 5 3 1

FIRST U.S. EDITION

Book design by Dana Leigh Blanchette

To my luminous children,
Poppy and Sam,

to my mother, Judy,
the lamp who has lit our family,

and to Jock,
who, herself, is
incandescence in the dark.

Phosphorescence. Now there's a word to lift your hat to. . . . To find that phosphorescence, that light within—is the genius behind poetry.

—EMILY DICKINSON

CONTENTS

Part II. We Are All Wiggly

Why we need to tell our imperfect stories

Part III. Walking Each Other Home

The art of friendship: "I am here"

Part IV. Invincible Summer

Regarde: Look, and savor

A Light Within

There are few things as startling as encountering an unearthly glow in the wild, in nature. Glow-worms. Ghost mushrooms. Fireflies. Flashlight fish. Lantern sharks. Vampire squid. Neon blue waves. Our forest floors and ceilings, our ocean depths and fringes are full of luminous beings, creatures lit from the inside. And they have, for many centuries, enchanted us, like glowing missionaries of wonder, emissaries of awe.

It turns out we glow in the dark too, faintly, even during the day. All living creatures do, apparently. In a study published in 2009, five healthy, bare-chested young Japanese men were placed in dark rooms sealed to keep light out, for twenty-minute intervals every three hours for three days. A highly sensitive imaging system found that all of the men glowed, most strongly from the face, at levels that dropped and climbed during the day. It's a small sample size, and the study does not seem to have been repeated, but it's a delicious thought.

The authors of the study, Masaki Kobayashi, Daisuke Kikuchi, and Hitoshi Okamura, concluded that we all "directly and rhythmically" emit light: "The human body literally glimmers. The intensity of the light emitted by the body is 1000 times lower than the sensitivity of our naked eyes."

Maybe we're all made of stardust.

. . .

A few years back, I was suffering heartbreak so intense I lost my appetite for months, and barely slept. I was skeletal, scattered, shorn of confidence. I called my counselor in tears and said, "I just don't know how I am going to get through this." He told me that, when he was a young man, he had once said exactly the same thing to a wise mentor of his. This man, an Argentinian, abruptly slapped him and said, "It is now that everything that you have been given in your life matters; this is what you draw on. Your parents, your friends, your work, your books, everything you have ever been told, everything you have ever learned, this is when you use that." And he was right. What is the point of all you have learned if you can't employ it when you are floundering in a nadir? Haven't all those lessons, and loves, been pooled in a reservoir you can draw on?

Since then, I have come close to death several times, and

now I often wonder why I let that old heartbreak send me into such orbital despair. In recent years, I have undergone brutal surgeries—three major ones—the most recent lasting for fifteen hours. I experienced at these times a kind of clarity and intensity of emotion that I had never known before: fear, anxiety, calm, loneliness, utter dread, love, an otherworldly focus. In the vortex of cancer, all other sounds get drowned out, and you hear only the beating of your heart, the drawing of your own breath, the uncertainty of your footfalls. You may be surrounded by the hugest crowd of family and friends, and by the shiniest love, but you walk alone through these medical valleys of darkness.

I have yearned for an end to excruciating pain that no drugs could touch, been haunted by opioid nightmares, spent months in hospital wards, and lain on my back in a surgical gown as hot, poisonous chemicals of chemotherapy were poured into a long open wound then swilled around. I have willed my body to work again after this venom paralyzed my insides, stumbling step by step and hobbling along corridors dragging a drip, trying to ensure my gown remained firmly fastened.

Of course, I know I am not the only one to have experienced this kind of trauma. We immediately understand each other, those of us who have staggered along the paths of serious sickness, but we also empathize more with other kinds of suffering—those millions of us with cracked hearts, battered bodies, blackened brains. We more readily commiserate about the times when life is like a boa constrictor wrapped around our windpipes, squeezing out breath; like a dark ogre stealing our joy, our purpose, and our hope as we sleep. Or sometimes it seems just like a thick, black airless cave with no apparent exit.

What has fascinated and sustained me over these past few years has been the notion that we have the ability to find, nurture, and carry our own inner, living light—a light to ward off the darkness. This is not about burning brightly; it's about yielding a more simple phosphorescence—being luminous at temperatures below incandescence, having stored light for later use, quietly glowing without combusting. Staying alive, remaining upright, even when lashed by doubt.

...

American author and marine biologist Rachel Carson discovered the phenomenon of living light as she waded around the shores of the Atlantic at night, shining a torch into dark waters. In August 1956, she wrote to her beloved friend Dorothy Freeman:

> There had been lots of swell and surf and noise all day, so it was most exciting down there toward midnight—all my rocks crowned with foam. . . . To get the full wildness, we turned off our flashlights— and then the real excitement began. The surf was full of diamonds and emeralds, and was throwing them on

the wet sand by the dozens. Dorothy, dear—it was the night we were there all over, but with everything intensified; a wilder accompaniment of noise and movement, and a great deal more phosphorescence. The individual sparks were so large—we'd see them glowing in the sand, or sometimes, caught in the in-and-out play of water, just riding back and forth. And several times I was able to scoop one up in my hand in shells and gravel, and think surely it was big enough to see— but no such luck.

What was also astounding for Carson that night was that she saw a firefly hovering over the water, his reflection "like a little headlight," and it dawned on her that he thought the sparkles in the water were other fireflies. She rescued him from drowning in the ice-cold sea, putting him in a bucket to dry his wings. The woman whose later work *Silent Spring* would ignite the modern environmental movement wrote: "It was one of those experiences that gives an odd and hard-to-describe feeling, with so many overtones beyond the facts themselves. . . . Imagine putting that in scientific language!" Indeed.

The language that scientists used to describe this other-worldly occurrence had changed through the centuries as their understanding of it grew. Light released by natural substances or organisms (usually reemitting absorbed heat like sunlight over a long period) had been known as "phospho-rescence" since the 1770s; in the early twentieth century the term "bioluminescence" was coined to specifically describe biochemical light emitted by living creatures, often phyto-plankton (which can look like "red tides" of algae during the day) stirred up by waves or motion in water. Some scientists—like Carson—still used the words interchangeably.

Before science explained the phenomenon of phospho-rescence in its various forms, it was the stuff of myth and legend. Aristotle puzzled over damp wood that glowed in the dark. The Japanese imagined fireflies to be the souls of the dead, or, more specifically, of samurai killed in battle. Sailors on ships gliding through luminescent blooms thought the waves were on fire; they spoke of "burning seas," "milky oceans," or "smoldering coals" on the water; Aristotle re-ferred to "exhalations of fire from the sea." In 1637, French philosopher René Descartes saw seawater "generate sparks rather similar to those which are emitted by pieces of flint when they are struck." In 1688, French Jesuit missionary Père Tachard declared the sparks were a consequence of the sun impregnating the sea by day with "an infinity of fiery and luminous spirits," and these spirits uniting after dark "to pass out in a violent state." Some observers, watching light trails spinning out from bows in the Indian Ocean, called them "the Wheels of Poseidon."

For me, today, these lights are the perfect metaphor for flashes of life in the middle of the dark, or joy in difficult times. But in centuries past, they were sheer magic. Charles Darwin was awestruck when he saw, while sailing through the Río de la Plata in the South Atlantic in 1845, "a sea that presented a wonderful and most beautiful spectacle. . . . The vessel drove before her bows two billows of liquid phosphorous, and in her wake she was followed by a milky train. As far as the eye reached the crest of every wave was bright, and the sky above the horizon, from the reflected glare of the livid flames, was not so utterly obscure as over the vault of the heavens."

No one attempted to seriously understand these mysterious sights until after World War I. During the conflict, tiny natural lights in the sea inadvertently aided war efforts by illuminating submarines: In November 1918, British naval officers sailing off the coast of Spain spied a large outline beneath them glowing and outlined by "sea fire," and attacked. This was the last German U-boat submarine to be destroyed in the war.

During World War II, the Japanese devised a clever way of illuminating maps with a light so faint that it would not alert enemies to their presence. Their army harvested vast piles of crustaceans called *umihotaru*, or ostracods—also known as sea fireflies—from the waters surrounding their country, and distributed them to their fighting units. The soldiers then needed only to hold these dried plankton in their hands, trickle liquid onto them, and crush them to obtain light. Scientist Osamu Shimomura said: "It was an easy, simple source of light. You just add water. Very convenient. You don't need any batteries." More than fifty years later, Shimomura—who won a Nobel Prize in 2008 for his work on green fluorescent protein in jellyfish—was able to produce the same effect for a colleague in a darkened room, clenching his fist then opening it to reveal a cool blue light.

By this time, both America and Russia had begun to study luminous creatures in earnest. In the 1960s, the U.S. Naval Oceanographic Office published a seminal study, relying on centuries of shipping records and journals in which naval officers struggled to describe what they saw. You can hear the gasp and wonder in their words, the fumbling for language adequate to describe the scenes. The lights were said to be like "a mass of boiling turquoise foam," "a luminous serpent," a "welding torch," "the illuminated dial of a wrist-watch," "magnesium burning." One witness reported being able to read on deck at night, due to the bright white light of the sea, "like that from molten iron."

Stories of these sightings had circled the globe for as long as ships had done the same: "spark-type displays" in the Gulf of Maine in summer; "green fire" strong enough to enter the portholes of a ship in Chesapeake Bay and "reflect from the ceiling of a stateroom"; "red tides" off the coast of Florida and Texas that turned luminescent at night; glowing waters in the Canary Islands; sea like a "star spangled sky" in the western Mediterranean basin; "flashes of light" in broken ice off the west coast of Norway; "sparkling emerald dots" in the Orkney Islands; glowing balls in the Thames; green oar strokes in the Irish Sea. In False Bay, off Cape Town, South Africa, what seemed a "greasy froth" by day was a lake of "molten gold" at night. When a tsunami receded at night near Sanriku, on the island of Honshu in Japan, "The exposed bottom was strongly luminescent with a bluish white light of such strength that land objects were visible as in daylight."

Myriad attempts have been made to measure and harness bioluminescence over the past few decades. But, while the U.S. Navy continues to study it today, and is reportedly attempting to develop an undersea robot that can track and monitor bioluminescence to help war efforts, work on its predictability and potential usefulness has never achieved the hoped-for broadscale harnessing of light, nature proving hard in this regard to bend to our will. In Roman times, the philosopher Pliny the Elder claimed it was possible to transform a walking stick into a torch by wiping the end with jellyfish paste, but this does not appear to have caught on. The ingenuity of Indigenous Indonesians in employing bioluminescent mushrooms as lights in the forest does not appear to have been replicated, either. On land, attempts by miners to light caverns with bottles filled with fireflies or phosphorescent dried fish skins were also unsuccessful.

Nevertheless, researchers are still trying to fathom how to use light-producing creatures, whether fireflies, fungi, or bacteria, for street, decorative, or domestic lights. There are hopes that bacteria like a genetically engineered form of the intestinal *E. coli* will be able to produce enough light to replace electricity in a "biobulb." Some scientists are even more ambitious. In biomedicine, living light is incredibly important: Scientists tweak and yoke various genes from jellyfish, coral, and fireflies to light up cancer cells and nerve cells, and to test drugs and monitor biochemical reactions.

But there's something gratifying about knowing such natural wonders cannot be completely plundered or exploited, particularly for the purpose of destruction. Today, sightings of living light remain rare, magical, and often unpredictable. Consequently, some people devote years to hunting it, seeing it, and recording it. In recent years, I became one of them.

• • •

Every now and then you actually do encounter someone who glows: someone who radiates goodness and seems to effortlessly inhabit a kind of joy, or seems so hungry for experience, so curious and engaged and fascinated with the world outside their head, that they brim with life, or light. These people are simultaneously soothing and magnetic.

The punk musician Henry Rollins proudly told me that he gets "tired but never jaded." Talking to him is like sticking a fork into an electrical socket—you walk away infected with his craving to do, know, and be more, to span seas and conquer weakness and fight for the rights of those who cannot, or should not be forced to, fight for themselves.

Tired, but not jaded. Yet it's hard to hold on to that glow. And very often life seems to snuff it out. So how can we find bellows to blow air on fire and fan flames? What can be done to nurture our inner lights, and guard them as jealously as an Olympian does a burning torch?

In recent years, those studying the still-nascent science of happiness have tapped into our cells, probed the flow of blood to our hearts and brains, and measured the variables in our daily moods to try to find what brings contentment, well-being, and joy. And now we have a few well-established core truths. Being altruistic makes us happy, as do turning off devices, talking to people, forging relationships, living with meaning, having a purpose, and delving into the concerns of others. Eating good food and going for a few runs, swims, or workouts help, too.

This is all very well if you are healthy, fit, and strong, or in a harmonious relationship, certain about the future and your family. But are we in fact asking the wrong question — instead of how do we stay happy, should we ask how do we survive, stay alive, or even bloom when the world goes dark, when we are, for instance, overwhelmed by illness or heartbreak, loss or pain? Is it possible to experience what monk David Steindl-Rast calls "that kind of happiness that doesn't depend on what happens"? When our days are shadowed and leached of meaning, when circumstances shower us with mud, how can we be sure to reemit lessons we absorb in the sunlight?

· · ·

In my own particularly dark days, when my world imploded with loss and illness, and when I had to find and tap into my own reserves, my search for what makes us phosphorescent took on a new urgency—and brought me immense beauty. In my quest for what Emily Dickinson called "the light within," I went in search of information and inspiration about phosphorescence and bioluminescence, and I learned to deliberately seek out awe and to find it in nature, in others, in friendship, in silence. I realized again a few simple, powerful lessons.

To find in nature a kind of daily rebirth. To pay attention.

To not underestimate the soothing power of the ordinary.

And also so many other things: show kindness, practice grace, eschew vanity, be bold, cherish those you love, embrace faith and doubt, let go of the idea of perfection, honor all of your own genuine strivings and mess, and live deliberately.

To my delight, I have found a burgeoning body of science that provides a substantial evidentiary basis for this kind of living phosphorescence. I know there are no surefire panaceas, of course, and a number of these recommendations may seem obvious to some readers, but when you stare down death then return to life, such beliefs take on a new clarity and urgency: You do not—you *cannot*—waste a breath.

. . .

This book is about my search for the "light within," for what makes people shine. The findings I have gathered here are not definitive, or comprehensive, but they struck me powerfully, and I wish I had understood them better when I was younger. Life is tempestuous and life is precious, and recognizing that those two things are twinned is part of the secret of the truly phosphorescent. That, and hunting awe.

PART I

Awe, Wonder, and Silence

In the company of the mysterious:
on forest therapy

"The most beautiful thing we can experience," wrote Albert Einstein, "is the mysterious; it is the source of all true art and all science. He to whom this emotion is a stranger, who can no longer pause to wonder and stand rapt in awe, is as good as dead; his eyes are closed." Being awestruck dwarfs us, humbles us, makes us aware we are part of a universe unfathomably larger than ourselves; it even, social scientists say, makes us kinder and more aware of the needs of the community around us.

Wonder is a similar sensation, and the two feelings are often entwined. Awe makes us stop and stare. Wonder makes us stop and ask questions about the world, while marveling over something we have not seen before, whether spectacular or mundane. The eighteenth-century Scottish moral philosopher Adam Smith—the man who became known as "the father of capitalism" after writing his influential book on economics, *The Wealth of Nations*—put this perfectly.

He thought wonder occurred "when something quite new and singular is presented . . . [and] memory cannot, from all its stores, cast up any image that nearly resembles this strange appearance. . . . It stands alone and by itself in the imagination." Smith believed that sometimes we could physically feel this wonder: "that staring, and sometimes that rolling of the eyes, that suspension of the breath, and that swelling of the heart."

Great thinkers, philosophers, and eccentrics have all been inspired by the mysterious, the unfathomable. In my own quest to become phosphorescent—in which I lost myself many times in dark holes and swamps—it was awe and wonder that I kept returning to, and the quiet healing properties of nature. I write about these things in this book, about the forest, the sea, and the creatures they contain.

So many of us have our quiet places of escape and refuge—nearby beaches, a park bench, a magnificent tree. Mine is most usually the sea, something as wild and raw as it is vast and beautiful. One day recently, whilst swimming at sunrise, I began thinking about how Oscar Wilde described the dawn as like a "frightened girl" who crept along the "long and silent street . . . with silver sandaled feet." It suddenly struck me as so timid and British (although Wilde was an Irishman, he lived many years in London). In Australia, the dawn is an arsonist who pours petrol along the horizon, throws a match on it, and watches it burn.

The sun's rise and the sun's retreat bookend our days

with awe. We often take this kind of awe for granted, and yet it's something both modern scientists and ancient philosophers have told us not just to appreciate but to hunt.

In fact, a small mountain of studies in the field of nature science has repeatedly confirmed that the sheer sight of green—plants, leaves, trees, views from windows—can make us happier and healthier. This evidence and these experiences have given rise to the burgeoning Japanese-pioneered practice of forest bathing, or *shinrin-yoku*, whereby participants are walked slowly through tracts of trees to touch them, listen to their sounds, and reconnect with nature. As scuba divers and free divers well know, similar experiences can be had when wandering through undersea forests; you slow, focus your gaze, and worlds open up to you.

All over the world, people increasingly want to understand how residents of an urbanized environment can tune out the cities, the traffic, and the jackhammers and listen, once again, to the birds singing and the leaves tossing in the breeze. They want to settle the stirring, or restlessness, and remember who they are. Often, they seek silence, an increasingly valuable and rare commodity. Real silence is not about muffling all sounds, though, but about muffling all artificial, or human-made, sounds. As I learned on a visit to Arnhem Land, a connection to country is a fundamental part of the identity of our Indigenous people, and the call to quiet, to listen and to respect the world we live in, is an ancient one. While so much of our self-exploration today is hash-tagged #wellness and displayed online, it became obvious to me in the far reach of sacred lands, encircled by campfires and eucalypts, that sometimes the best way to pay attention to country is to keep your mouth shut, open your eyes, and just listen.

CHAPTER 1

Lessons from a Cuttlefish

Those who dwell, as scientists or laymen, among the beauties or mysteries of the earth are never alone or weary of life. . . . Their thoughts can find paths that lead to inner contentment and to renewed excitement in living. Those who contemplate the beauty of the earth find reserves of strength that will endure as long as life lasts.

— RACHEL CARSON, *THE SENSE OF WONDER*

The first time I saw a cuttlefish swimming in the wild I was astounded by how prehistoric and alien it looked. Cuttlefish are astonishing creatures, with heads like an elephant's, eight arms they occasionally splay then join together like a trunk, and small bodies ringed with thin, rippling fins that look like a silk shawl. They glide across the ocean floor, changing their color to match the surface underneath them, from gold above sand to brown and red over seaweed, and even their texture, from smooth to thorny, blends in with the background so effectively that they are often noticeable only when they move their silken frills.

Cuttlefish are not just otherworldly in appearance. Consider these facts: Their pupils are shaped like the letter "W," and it has been speculated that cuttlefish eyes are fully developed before birth and that the young start observing their surroundings while still in the egg. Their blood is colorless until exposed to air, when it turns blue-green. They have three hearts and a doughnut-shaped brain that is larger in proportion to its body size than that of any other invertebrate. The cuttlefish bone—a white oval-shaped object often seen washed up on beaches or in parakeet cages—is actually a thick, calcified internal shell that helps cuttlefish control flotation, and separates them from fellow cephalopods such as squids and octopuses. There are four or five male cuttlefish for every female—an excellent ratio in my view—but all live for only a year or two.

For me, cuttlefish are symbols of awe. After my first sighting, I was charged with a peculiar kind of electricity for hours. They still have this effect on me. I regularly spend the winter admiring them, then mourn when the spring tides cast their light white bones onto the shore.

When I dive down to swim alongside cuttlefish, as I have several times this week, the world slows to the rhythm of ruffling skin. They rarely flee and are sometimes quite friendly. Seeing them regularly in the bay at the foot of my hill has given me an unexpected insight into awe. If I had guessed that spying them gliding along reefs could be part of my daily ritual, I would have devoted myself to ocean swimming decades ago.

Peter Godfrey-Smith, a professor of philosophy and history, who also lives on my hill, likens the giant cuttlefish, which can grow to a meter in length, to "an octopus attached to a hovercraft" with arms like "eight huge and dexterous lips." He reminds us that "the mind evolved in the sea. All the early stages took place in water: the origin of life, the birth of animals, the evolution of nervous systems and brains, and the appearance of the complex bodies that make brains worth having. . . . When animals did crawl onto dry land, they took the sea with them. All the basic activities of life occur in water-filled cells bounded by membranes, tiny containers whose insides are remnants of the sea." In other words, the sea is inside us.

. . .

If you joined the hundreds of people in my swim squad, you might think at first that the routine was simply about getting a solid bout of exercise before the day begins. We meet after sunrise at Sydney's Manly Beach, swim out to the headland, then arc across a protected marine bay to another beach.

The caps we wear are bright pink. The name we call ourselves, the Bold and Beautiful, is a bit daft, but it's a reminder that the squad was formed years ago by middle-aged women who were too nervous to swim the distance alone. This morning swim was never about skill, but about pluck.

Most days, at some spot along the mile-long route, heads will cluster, arms pointing down under the water at enormous blue gropers, cuttlefish in various states of disguise (also occasionally breeding, or devouring each other), bearded wobbegongs, Port Jackson sharks, eagle rays, and even tiny darting turtles and seahorses. Just this week, a pod of dolphins curved past me as I swam around the headland.

In early winter, dozens of young dusky whaler sharks usually swarm the bay, only a few meters beneath us, migrating only after they have become large enough to make people nervous—there's a reason a collective term for sharks is a "shiver." (While I was writing this, a dawn swimmer was bitten by a shark he says he bumped into in the dark sea while he wasn't wearing a headlight. The fact that it was a usually mild gray nurse shark meant we were able to continue swimming without fear.)

One day, a whale glided into the bay and played with the swimmers for an hour—though I refuse to talk about it because I wasn't there. (I had to read about it instead in *The Daily Telegraph*, under the headline A WHALE OF A DAY.) My atheist friends who were there described it as like a prayer or quasi-religious experience; their faces turned solemn at the recollection. Okay, whatever.

Our outings are not always ideal. Frequently we battle thickets of seaweed, powerful currents, and daunting, crashing waves that pull you under and spin you around, or dump you against the sandy floor. Occasionally the swell is so big, and the undertow so strong, that I make sure I am with a friend as I swim back to shore. Newcomers often need to be rescued. Sometimes we emerge with red welts from stingers across our faces and limbs. I will never forget the swarms of jimbles—small, box-shaped jellyfish with long, trailing pink tentacles—that inhabited the bay in the thousands for many months one year. Though we put on protective wetsuits and smeared our faces, hands, and feet with pawpaw ointment, many people still bear the scars of their stings and some even landed in hospital. But the daily difference in conditions is what makes it thrilling.

Something happens when you dive into a world where clocks don't tick and in-boxes don't ping. As your arms circle, swing, and pull along the edge of a vast ocean, your mind wanders, and you open yourself to awe—to the experience of seeing something astonishing, unfathomable, or greater than yourself. Studies have shown that awe can make us more patient and less irritable, more humble, more curious and creative—even when just watching nature documentaries. It can ventilate and expand our concept of time: Researchers Melanie Rudd, Kathleen Vohs, and Jennifer Lynn Aaker found that "experiences of awe bring people into the present moment, and being in the present moment underlies awe's capacity to adjust time perception, influence decisions, and make life feel more satisfying than it would otherwise."

Research conducted by social psychologist Paul Piff and

his colleagues suggests that people who regularly feel awe are more likely to be generous, helpful, altruistic, ethical, and relaxed. In one case, people who spent time staring up at towering eucalypts were more inclined to help someone who had stumbled and dropped a handful of pens than those who had not. In other words, when dwarfed by an experience, we are more likely to look to one another and care for one another and feel more connected.

It would be wrong to think of exercise only as something to build muscle and ease anxiety. If we can, we should force ourselves out of gyms and off machines and into the natural world, knowing, or hoping, that we may stumble upon awe.

. . .

Those of us in our squad hardly need research to tell us about the joys and benefits of ocean swimming. Several of my Bold and Beautiful friends have stopped taking antidepressants: They call the ocean "vitamin sea." One, who documents the creatures of the teeming bay with gloriously lit photographs, calls the swim her "happy pill." Others use it to survive: Several fellow swimmers going through illness, breakups, or family traumas have told me how they have cried into blurry goggles while swimming around the headland, before returning to hot showers and coffee, able to garner strength for another day.

As Wallace J. Nichols, author of *Blue Mind*, a book about

the benefits of being in or near water, says, water "meditates *you*." A study published in the *British Medical Journal* in August 2018 posited the theory that swimming in cold, open water could be a treatment for depression, which is again science starting to catch up with what we already know — why else would I find myself, a night owl, rising before dawn to jump into black seas if it wasn't an addictive high? The study was based on the experience of a twenty-four-year-old woman who found that a weekly swim in cold water allowed her to stop her medication. The authors were uncertain why this happened. One suggestion was that the water worked as an anti-inflammatory or treatment for pain; however, the explanation that rang true for me was a theory put forward by co-author Michael Tipton: "If you adapt to cold water, you also blunt your stress response to other daily stresses such as road rage, exams or getting fired at work."

The awe found in daily group swims does bring a sense of connection, as does the companionship. We are a strong community, a motley crew bound by a common love. The conversations of our diverse crowd — which includes judges, carpenters, models, priests, doctors, care workers, and teachers, and ranges in age from five-year-olds who paddle on boards to veterans in their eighties — are also part of the cheerfully repeated daily ritual. We talk about the beauty of the sunrise, the presence of stinging jellyfish, the creatures we spied on the ocean floor or hidden in the weeds, whether a wetsuit is needed, the weather, the water temperature, the visibility, and the swell. And we complain about how long it takes for the local café to make our hot drinks. Then we have the same conversations the following day.

In an era of increasing disconnection, digital-only relationships, and polarization of political views, it is wonderful to sit among such a varied group of people—with many of whom you really share only one thing—and talk rubbish and riptides. I walk down the stairs at the south end of the beach each day knowing that I will see dozens of beaming faces before I put a toe in the water, and that each of them knows how lucky they are to have, and to share, this experience. Often we hold bake sales or fundraisers for the local surf club or various charities. When I came back from the hospital, for months members of the swim group would drop meals on my doorstep, walk my dog, feed the cat, plant trees in my garden, and do all manner of things, unasked.

The importance of daily contact with people—the old-fashioned face-to-face kind—has been well documented by researchers, including American sociologist Robert Putnam, who lamented the decline in America of social organizations such as churches, unions, and community groups in his 2000 book *Bowling Alone: The Collapse and Revival of American Community.* In recent years, the number of people who say they have very few or no confidants or close friends has rocketed, with worrying implications for our well-being: Greater isolation and loneliness have been linked to increased risk of chronic illness and dementia, alcohol abuse, sleep problems, obesity, diabetes, hypertension, poor hearing, and depression.

A sense of community can also make us more resilient, not only improving our current state of mind but also protecting our mental health in the future. One of the world's longest studies of adult life, the Harvard Study of Adult Development, followed subjects for eighty years—beginning in 1938—and found that social connection and relationships are the single greatest predictor of health and happiness throughout your life. (The headline of a recent piece in *The Harvard Gazette* describing the findings was GOOD GENES ARE NICE, BUT JOY IS BETTER.) The director of that study, Robert Waldinger, who is a professor of psychiatry at Harvard Medical School as well as a Zen priest, now ensures he deliberately invests more time in his close relationships than he did previously. Another study, published in the *Australian & New Zealand Journal of Psychiatry* in 2017, concluded that the resources conferred by social connectedness can act as a "social cure" for "psychological ill-health."

Why then don't we all do more to foster a sense of community? It's hard when you're shy, or blue, or sick, or struggling—my own instinct is often to close the shutters and be quiet and solitary. But that instinct is not always the healthiest one. In order to endure, to survive trauma, or even just to stay afloat when life threatens to suck us under, we need to know we are not alone.

It's not just relationships with friends and family that

count: Connections with people who live on the same streets, work in the same offices, or ride the same trains as us also matter. A 2014 study by researchers at the University of British Columbia found that even interactions with "weak social ties" such as casual acquaintances—like members of a sporting club—were significant. Students who interacted with more classmates than usual on any given day reported being happier, for example.

I certainly know that the days I begin with casual conversations and a long swim in salt water are almost always better than those that don't start that way. Ask any swimmer or surfer. The memory stays in my mind and on my skin (and, unfortunately for the makeup artists who need to get me ready to host a nightly TV show, in goggle rings around my eyes). Other swimmers concur: If they don't have the chance to jump in the ocean before work, they are twitchier, less settled, and less focused than on the days when they do.

. . .

For a long stretch of time in my twenties, I preferred lamplight to sunlight. I wasn't gothic; I was nocturnal. I danced marathons under lasers and mirrored globes in lambent clubs and strobe-lit warehouses. But outside, along the rim of Australia's broad coastline, I hunted for sunlight trapped in water. At the end of the week, my friends and I would throw tents into car trunks and drive north of Sydney for several hours until we reached, in darkness, a place called Seal Rocks. Painted in large white letters on the road that curved down to the ocean were the words THE LAST FRONTIER.

The beach there was unspoiled, untamed, brimming with wildlife. We'd park our cars and run into the black sea, diving and swirling under the moon, watching a silvery, sparkling ribbon of phosphorescence trail behind our limbs. The tiny little sea creatures that absorbed the light of the sun were stirred up by our thrashing; we found we were streaming sequins, or galaxies of bioluminescence, in our wake. In truth they were phytoplankton that were reacting chemically to movement—generating energy from sunlight (photosynthesis) to drive light-producing chemical reactions when stirred up—but to us it seemed magical. These living lights became a kind of symbol of joy and abandon for me, and I tried to find more ways to experience them, and companions who would love them as much as I did.

• • •

There are several sacred aspects to how Australians submit to the sea. First is the way we are drawn to it, gazing out at its expanses, and lie down near it whenever we can. Second is the purifying ritual of plunging, and third is immersing ourselves in it and exploring its subterranean secrets. A fourth may be the surfer's learned respect for its thunderous swells, tides, and curling waves. Chlorinated pools will never have the same charm as the wide blue sea; a pool lane's black line can become hypnotic but is also dull, and the water is heavy with chemicals.

After first having major surgery, I yearned to slip back into the sea. When I finally rejoined the Manly Beach group, I practically danced for the rest of the day. As my shoulders began to grow stronger, so did my mind. Swimming is a form of meditation. As the amazing Diana Nyad, who in 2013, at the age of sixty-four, became the first person to swim from Cuba to Florida without the protection of a shark cage, told *The New York Times*, swimming is the ultimate way to deprive your senses: "You are left alone with your thoughts in a much more severe way."

Sound is diminished, yes. But, for me, ocean swimming is the ultimate way to expand my senses—of sight, space, and subdued sounds—and heighten my awareness. Afterward, through my working day, images of a rippled sea floor and bearded sharks flash through my thoughts. I collect and recount underwater sightings for my children as a hunter would collect skins.

A swim is a reminder of the vastness of the ocean and all it contains. We spend a lot of time in life trying to make ourselves feel bigger—to project ourselves, occupy space, command attention, demand respect—so much so that we seem to have forgotten how comforting it can be to feel small and experience the awe that comes from being silenced by something greater than ourselves, something unfathomable, unconquerable, and mysterious.

This sense of smallness seems to be a key to a true experience of awe, and in turn to linking with others. Attempting to provide an academic definition of awe, social psychologists Dacher Keltner and Jonathan Haidt wrote: "Two appraisals are central and are present in all clear cases of awe: perceived vastness, and a need for accommodation, defined as an inability to assimilate an experience into current mental structures." They pointed out that architects of religious structures have always attempted to engender a sense of smallness, and consequently awe, by designing buildings on a grand scale: soaring ceilings, domed canopies, enormous columns, vast stained-glass windows. During his research, Paul Piff noted that people who stood near an enormous T. rex skeleton subsequently more strongly identified as being in a group, possibly because they viewed themselves differently when shadowed by a huge—if extinct—beast.

In one study of American and Chinese people, Keltner found that after experiencing awe, people signed their names in tinier letters. He told *New Scientist* magazine that the reason for this is that "awe produces a vanishing self. The voice in your head, self-interest, self-consciousness, disappears. Here's an emotion that knocks out a really important part of our identity. . . . I think the central idea of awe is to quiet self-interest for a moment and to fold us into the social collective."

This is also what we sense when we swim in the sea. We become small. When we shrink in significance, we become better at living alongside and caring for others. And we become more content.

. . .

Fortunately, cultivating awe does not have to mean daily ocean dives, annual trips to see the northern lights, or bungee jumping in the Grand Canyon. One of the more reassuring findings of recent research is how commonly awe can be found: in museums, theaters, parks, ponds, while listening to a street performer, or even, surprisingly, in micro doses, while witnessing acts of great generosity, watching an acrobat, marveling at the feats of an elite athlete, or reading a story. Amie Gordon from Berkeley tracked people's reports of awe for two weeks and found that on average, they encountered something that inspired awe every three days, such as "music played on a street corner at 2 A.M., individuals standing up to injustice, or autumnal leaves cascading from trees."

Today, scientists are trying to measure awe by goosebumps. (Only cold, adrenaline, or strong emotion are more likely to cause goosebumps in a human being.) In an increasingly awe-deprived culture, when we are more likely to get lost in our screens than in the woods or public galleries, when we hedge our children's explorations with our anxieties and fears, it seems increasingly vital that we deliberately seek out such experiences whenever we can. The good news is that they are very often all around us, in every corner of nature.

CHAPTER 2

"A Better Show Outside"

In the woods . . . all mean egotism vanishes. I become
a transparent eyeball.

— RALPH WALDO EMERSON, "NATURE"

The man known as the father of American storm chasing
was in a movie theater in Bismarck, North Dakota, in the
summer of 1956 when his obsession began. David Hoadley
had seen a red-gold sun setting under a darkening cloud as
he walked in to take a seat, and he heard the sound of cracking thunder after the movie started. Then his father tore
into the theater and told him there was "a better show outside." They drove around darkened streets, past felled cot-
tonwood trees and power lines as skies flickered with
lightning, then rounded a corner to see "a bare plot of grass,
where a broken—but live—power line flashed bright, hot

sparks, and jumped like a snake in the wet grass." The city was black, but the sky blazed with light.

Hoadley was hooked. The next day he explored the town to inspect the damage and saw a transmission tower doubled over as though in pain, the top end on the ground. Lacking the technology today's storm chasers rely upon to track the skies, Hoadley began to study the weather in an intense and methodical fashion, creating elaborate charts, plotting surface maps, and trying to find patterns in morning data that could help predict the nature of afternoon storms.

Storm chasers are addicted to awe. In what seem like secular pilgrimages, they drive for thousands of miles to pursue, map, snap, report, record, or just gawk and gaze at severe weather events. These tend to be, most spectacularly, tornadoes, but include thunderstorms, dust storms, cyclones, waterspouts, and rare cloud formations like mammatus or shelf clouds.

Although what they are pursuing are frequently horrendously destructive events, chasers often speak in poetry, using words and phrases like "anvil," "ghost," "cell," "squall," "fire devil," "dust devil," "willy-willy," "tower," "radar," "lift," "wind shear," "thunderhead," and "core-punching." They spend weeks at a time thundering along isolated roads, eyes straining for shifts in cloud patterns and winds and the most diabolical storms, the supercells that give rise to the most spectacular, long-lasting tornadoes and other dramatic formations. There is a kind of a religiosity to their obsession.

Australian Nick Moir, a superb photographer, has been chasing extreme weather for twenty years, in Australia and the United States. He sees storms as "living entities," or giant animals, each one unique. A former colleague of mine at *The Sydney Morning Herald*, where he is now chief photographer, Moir long ago earned the reputation of being a driven risk-taker. In May 2019, while chasing storms around the town of Imperial, Nebraska, he saw what he believed to be the "most beautiful [storm] cell of the decade," in a storm that was subsequently dubbed the "Imperial Mothership." Watching the atmosphere swirl around the storm was "awe-inspiring," he said. "It's like looking at a god. When clouds, the atmosphere becomes so organized . . . it's no wonder people thought these things were deities. I took a lot of shots, but I also just stood and watched it. It's rotating in real time, this thing that's 30 to 50 kilometers across. It's like the spaceship from *Independence Day*."

Awe can fuel adrenaline, but it is the result of more than danger, risk, and speed: It is about witnessing something spectacular and rare. As Moir has said, chasing storms "makes you feel really small. . . . It reminds us of how insignificant we are." In the short film *Chasing Monsters* by Krystle Wright, Moir is shown crying out "Look at it!" as he stands with his curly hair whipping his face, in front of an enormous, looming, swirling dark cloud. He throws his arms wide while bending his knees, as though in prayer, a man worshipping over and over, "Look at it! Look at iiiiiit!

This is why we come here." Wright, who was with Moir on the day of the Imperial Mothership, said it was "utterly surreal": "I felt the full range of emotions from fear to ecstasy."

It is a range of emotions that inspires addiction—one David Hoadley, now an octogenarian, is very familiar with. In 1977, Hoadley, who worked as a budget analyst in the water-quality program at the Environmental Protection Authority, founded *Storm Track* magazine, which allowed the diverse community of storm chasers to communicate for the first time. A few years later, in *Storm Track*, he tried to answer the question most frequently asked of storm chasers: "Why?" He wrote: "First is the sheer, raw experience of confronting an elemental force of nature—uncontrolled and unpredictable—which is at once awesome, magnificent, dangerous and picturesque. Few life experiences can compare with the anticipation of a chaser while standing in the path of a big storm, in the gusty inflow of warm, moist gulf wind sweeping up into a lowering, darkening cloud base, grumbling with thunder as a great engine begins to turn."

Then there was the "experience of something infinite, a sense of powers at work and scales of movement that so transcend a single man and overwhelm the senses that one feels intuitively (without really seeking) something eternal—but ephemeral—almost a conscious thought, but just below the surface. As when a vertical 50,000-foot wall of clouds glides silently away to the east (intermittent, distant thunder) and goes golden in a setting sun against a deep, rich azure sky, one can only pause and look and wonder."

Hoadley is sometimes called the "pioneer" storm chaser because he was the first to travel interstate while chasing, and to make his own predictions. He, however, defers to a man called Roger Jensen, who began actively hunting and photographing severe thunderstorms a little earlier. Jensen began chasing in 1953 when still a teenager, but saw his first tornado in Fargo in 1957: "a big and dirty thunderstorm backlit by the sun."

Today storm chasing has become cool, with inevitable consequences: Roads surrounding storm systems are increasingly choked with TV and radio crews, amateur photographers, adrenaline junkies, and safari-type storm-chasing tours, as well as veteran chasers, who roll their eyes at the embarrassing commercialization and the yahoos who don't understand the dangers and are prone to be reckless. Of these new adherents, Jensen said, sounding doubtful, "I hope they are out chasing for the same reasons we are chasing."

According to *Storm Track*, while most chasers are steeped in meteorology and forecasting, they come from a broad range of professions, including roofers, postal workers, pilots, and store owners. Ninety-eight percent are men, and the average age is thirty-five. For some, storm chasing is a thrill, for others a thirst.

For those who are truly dedicated, it's not a fad, but an all-consuming love. Jensen was succinct when asked why he had chased storms for fifty years: "Gosh, it's for the awe at what you're seeing. I was born loving storms." To support his passion, he worked in his farm and greenhouse, as well as at a turkey-processing plant. In the years before he died, in 2001, he and his friends ensured he found a nursing home in Texas that had an "unobstructed vantage point."

. . .

Few of us actually live in Tornado Alley, which is doubtless a relief for some. Many people would travel distances to *avoid* terrifying extreme weather events, which, scientists predict, are unfortunately going to occur more frequently in the future as a result of climate change. This fact alone makes the role of photography even more important, in documenting the often-devastating consequences of changing weather patterns. Moir, for example, has been chasing and photographing dust storms, too—as well as Australia's cataclysmic bushfires—which is one crucial way of recording the impact of drought in rural Australia.

It's not necessary, though, to go accelerating into storm systems to experience the awe and wonder associated with weather phenomena; we can often savor it in our own suburbs, even our own gardens. Which is why I love the story of Clyve Herbert, an Australian who spent two decades chasing big storms in the outback without luck, then finally saw a tornado when he was hanging out the washing in his backyard. Herbert, who lives on the Bellarine Peninsula, southwest of Melbourne, told *The Age*, "I just noticed a funnel hanging out the back of a storm. I raced inside, got my camera and chased the tornado on foot. My children were going berserk, running around like field mice!"

. . .

Even today, awe and wonder are underexplored emotions— those feelings of being amazed, overwhelmed, quieted, or surprised by something truly extraordinary, magical: the wonder of a black hole, cauliflower clouds, the slash of lightning, a blue sky, neon scales, curling cyclones, roaring meteors, tiny petals, feathers arced in flight.

The sense of awe and wonder engendered by such natural phenomena is a fishhook for curiosity. Take rainbows, for instance. For millennia humans have tried to understand the startling magic of rainbows. In dozens of myths and legends they were depicted as an archer's bow, a snake, a bridge. For Christians, rainbows have long been a sign of God's grace, and a promise that the Earth would never again be destroyed by a global flood. For Buddhists, the rainbow body is the highest state achievable before attaining Nirvana. In some countries, the sight of a colorful bow spanning the skies was a fearful one: Children scurried into hiding places to avoid looking directly at it (in Honduras and Nicaragua) or being eaten by a demon (in Myanmar); elsewhere, people closed their mouths, men nervously girded their loins.

In Bulgaria, the superstitious said that if you walked under a rainbow, you would change genders, immediately starting to think like a man if you were a woman, and a woman if you were a man. In ancient Japan, Hawaii, and Greece, rainbows served as bridges between the heavens and the Earth, the ancestors and the gods. For Indigenous Australians, the sacred rainbow snake represents the life-giving creator.

The first modern thinker to study rainbows—and show how they occur—was the French philosopher, mathematician, and eccentric genius René Descartes, who believed that wonder was the greatest of the passions. In 1628, when living in the Netherlands and studying metaphysics, he heard about the spectacular appearance of a host of false suns—known as sun dogs or parhelia—in the sky over Rome. He determined to study light, and rainbows followed. In 1637, Descartes wrote the oft-cited line *Cogito ergo sum*, or "I think therefore I am," in his book *Discourse on the Method*. What we rarely talk about is that in the same book, he provided what his biographer A. C. Grayling called "the first satisfactory explanation of rainbows," describing how airborne water, light, and refraction interact to conjure those extraordinary sights.

. . .

English philosopher Francis Bacon called wonder "broken knowledge," a gap in understanding that some race to fill, if they can. (Both Plato and Aristotle believed philosophy was rooted in wonder.) Wonder prompts us to ask questions of one another and the world. It is also an antidote to distraction. As Robert Fuller, professor of religious studies at Bradley University, argues in his fascinating book *Wonder: From Emotion to Spirituality*, the experience of wonder is "one of the defining elements of human spirituality." It fuels art, science, and religion. American philosophy professor Jesse Prinz describes this "wide-eyed, slack-jawed feeling" of wonder as "humanity's most important emotion."

The significance of awe and wonder is far broader than just maintaining our sanity. As American philosopher Martha Nussbaum, a professor of law and ethics at the University of Chicago, has argued, a core part of being human is wondering about creatures other than ourselves. And yet, these days, wonder seems to be on the wane, or we tend to wonder mainly about ourselves, instead of allowing wonder to lift us up out of our own self-interest and help us to understand others and the natural world better. Rachel Carson was concerned that "most of us walk unseeing through the world, unaware alike of its beauties, its wonders, and the strange and sometimes terrible intensity of the lives that are being lived around us." That's still true today. Even to catch a glimpse of another creature's suffering is to be humbled, sobered. And if we don't pay attention to the Earth, to each other, we all suffer. As it is, we are already bearing witness to a planet where rivers are choked with poison, rainbow corals are being bleached white, swallows are disappearing, and insects are vanishing.

Children understand awe and wonder as naturally as breathing. Yet we must also actively teach them to observe and wonder, says Nussbaum. It might begin with nursery rhymes. As Nussbaum writes in her essay "The Narrative Imagination":

> When a child and a parent begin to tell stories together, the child is acquiring essential moral capacities. Even a simple nursery rhyme such as "Twinkle, twinkle, little star, how I wonder what you are" leads children to feel wonder—a sense of mystery that mingles curiosity with awe. Children wonder about the little star. In so doing they learn to imagine that a mere shape in the heavens has an inner world, in some ways mysterious, in some ways like their own. They learn to attribute life, emotion, and thought to a form whose insides are hidden.

Singer and songwriter Nick Cave agrees with this approach, partly as a result of his belief that humans will always seek the transcendent. Given the ugliness of much of what we see online and hear in news bulletins, he says he has always seen it as a parental duty to show his own children "beautiful stuff, and in so doing reveal to them an alternative world."

Some of us need to teach ourselves how to wonder again, how to be ready for that sensation. When was the last time you had goosebumps? Or just bent to watch a bee at work, look at the tiny world contained in a rock pool, or closely trace a plant's hopeful trajectory from bud to bloom? Made sure you were able to stare at a full stretch of horizon, or regularly gave yourself time to gaze at the sunrises and sunsets that bracket our days with beauty? Mostly, all we have to do is pause and look. Just today, I noticed a yellow-tailed black cockatoo for the first time, swooping with a mate into a tree overhead, and swam over a diving bird called a cormorant, feathers splayed as it headed toward the surface, little stripey fish trapped in its beak. We both popped up to the surface at the same time, and I watched it stretch its neck: gulp.

Sometimes by seeking awe and wonder, we can open ourselves up to other experiences, too. David Hoadley, for example, would be sorely disappointed if he missed a nearby tornado, but said that often "after a few hours of dejected driving, the night sky would darken, clear itself of clouds, and a million sparkling diamonds would appear." He would then pull over on the side of the road, stop his car, "turn off the lights, look up—and begin healing, amidst wonders that make my small pain even smaller—until it disappears altogether. How can anything you say, or do, or feel matter beneath such stunning beauty and depth? This is also storm chasing."

...

Moonbows exist, too, and serve as a reminder that occasionally we can be blinkered, or blind to the wonder in front of us. For they are fainter and can seem plain white from a distance or in low light. Yet they are full of color.

It's possible to reveal the full spectrum of pigments in a moonbow using long-exposure photographs. You need to wait, and wait, and wait to draw out the vivid hues, and often only then will it become apparent that the full panoply of colors was there all along. You just could not see them in the dark.

CHAPTER 3

The Overview Effect

Surely the best witnesses to the fact that the key to awe and wonder is feeling small are astronauts. Like Captain Jim Lovell, who, when on board the Apollo 8 on Christmas Eve 1968, raised his hand against the window, and watched the entire planet disappear. "I realized how insignificant we all are if everything I'd ever known is behind my thumb," he said. The first person to ever step onto the moon, Neil Armstrong, did exactly the same thing. He recalled later: "It suddenly struck me that that tiny pea, pretty and blue, was the Earth. I put up my thumb and shut one eye, and my thumb blotted out the planet Earth. I didn't feel like a giant. I felt very, very small."

We have shot hundreds of human beings into space over the past few decades, most with a background in engineering, science, medicine, or the military, and almost all of them seem to return with permanently widened eyes. Former soldiers suddenly speak of elation, mathematicians of

bliss, biologists of transcendence. The term for the psychological impact of flying into space and viewing the Earth as
a simple dot is called "the overview effect," a term coined by
author Frank White in his book of the same name in 1987.
White defined it as "a profound reaction to viewing the
Earth from outside its atmosphere."

The overview effect turns astronauts into "evangelists,
preaching the gospel of orbit" as they return from space with
a renewed faith or on a quest for wisdom. For some it's a
kind of lingering euphoria that results in a permanent
change of perspective. The first human to reach outer space,
the Russian cosmonaut Yuri Gagarin, circled the Earth for
108 minutes in 1961 and came back with a clarion call: "Orbiting Earth in the spaceship, I saw how beautiful our planet
is. People, let us preserve and increase this beauty, not destroy it."

In recent years, scientists have been trying to measure
and understand the overview effect, even attempting to send
people into virtual space, where they view galaxies through
portals and are grilled about their responses, but the accounts of astronauts provide the best insights. The words
they use are saturated with awe, an understanding of how
fragile the Earth is, with its paper-thin atmosphere, and how
much needs to be done to protect it and its inhabitants.

As Syrian astronaut Muhammad Ahmad Faris said, when
you look at Earth from space, the "scars of national boundaries" disappear. American Sam Durrance said he became
emotional after having hurtled past the stratosphere into

black space because "you're removed from the Earth but at the same time you feel this incredible connection to the Earth like nothing I'd ever felt before." Mae Jemison, the first black woman to travel in space, who orbited the Earth 127 times in 1992 on board the space shuttle *Endeavor*, also says she felt "very connected with the rest of the universe." (She later told students: "Life is best when you live deeply and look up.")

The Japanese term *yūgen*, which derives from the study of aesthetics, is sometimes used to describe space gazing. It is said to mean "a profound, mysterious sense of the beauty of the universe . . . and the sad beauty of human suffering," though the meaning and translation depend on the context. Japanese actor and aesthetician Zeami Motokiyo described some of the ways to access *yūgen*:

To watch the sun sink behind a flower clad hill.

To wander on in a huge forest without thought of return. To stand upon the shore and gaze after a boat that disappears behind distant islands. To contemplate the flight of wild geese seen and lost among the clouds.

And, subtle shadows of bamboo on bamboo.

Or to stare at the heavens from Earth, or Earth from the heavens.

Yūgen is also defined as "an awareness of the universe that triggers emotional responses too big and powerful for words." It's striking how, repeatedly, people who venture into space speak of the inadequacy of words. Former NASA astronaut Kathryn D. Sullivan, who in 1984 became the first woman to ever walk in space (and in 2013 was nominated by President Obama to be under secretary of commerce for oceans and atmosphere), was also gobsmacked. "It's hard to explain how amazing and magical this experience is," she says. "First of all, there's the astounding beauty and diversity of the planet itself, scrolling across your view at what appears to be a smooth, stately pace. . . . I'm happy to report that no amount of prior study or training can fully prepare anybody for the awe and wonder this inspires."

American engineer and astronaut Nicole Stott reported that she was "stunned in a way that was completely unexpected." She described it to her seven-year-old son this way: "Just take a lightbulb—the brightest lightbulb that you could ever possibly imagine—and paint it all the colors that you know Earth to be, and turn it on, and be blinded by it."

When you shrink, your ability to see somehow sharpens. When you see the beauty, vastness, and fragility of nature, you want to preserve it. You see what we share. You understand being small. Cosmonaut Boris Volynov said that after seeing Earth from black space "you become more full of life, softer. You begin to look at all living things with greater trepidation and you begin to be more kind and patient with the people around you." Scott Kelly, who spent a full year on the International Space Station from 2015 to 2016, delighting Earth-dwellers with his tweets and superb photographs, told *Business Insider* that the experience of space makes people more empathetic, "more in touch with humanity and who we are, and what we should do to not only take care of the planet but also to solve our common problems, which clearly are many." Kelly's insights echo those of many others: the splendor and vulnerability of the Earth, the connectedness of people, and the need to work in concert, across nations. He said:

> The planet is incredibly beautiful, breathtakingly beautiful. Having said that, parts of it are polluted, like with constant levels of pollution in certain parts of Asia. You see how fragile the atmosphere looks. It's very thin. It's almost like a thin contact lens over somebody's eye, and you realize all the pollutants we put into the atmosphere are contained in that very thin film over the surface. It's a little bit scary actually to look at it.
>
> And then you realize looking at the Earth, that despite its beauty and its tranquility, there's a lot of hardship and conflict that goes on. You look at the planet without borders, especially during the day. At night you can see countries with lights, but during the daytime it looks like we are all part of one spaceship, Spaceship Earth.
>
> And we're all flying through space together, as a team, and it gives you this perspective—people have described it as this "orbital perspective"—on humanity, and you get this feeling that we just need to work

better—much, much better—to solve our common problems.

The first Canadian to walk in space, Chris Hadfield, says whizzing across continents and seeing a sunrise or sunset every forty-five minutes creates "a feeling of privilege and sort of a reverence, an awe that is pervasive. And that sense of wonder and privilege and clarity of the world slowly shifts your view." He believes the overview effect is not limited to spaceflight but is more about "when you sense that there is something so much bigger than you, so much more deep than you are, ancient, [that] has sort of a natural importance that dwarfs your own." This understanding, Hadfield suggests, can lead people to make smarter global decisions, and less "jealous, local, narrow" ones. We hope.

One of my favorite scientists is the brilliant Carl Sagan, an eloquent speaker, prolific author, and cosmologist who was known in America as "the astronomer of the people." He studied extraterrestrial life and sent physical "universal" messages into space in the hope that other beings might find and understand them. In his 1994 book *Pale Blue Dot*, which is about the solar system and our place in it, Sagan wrote about the sight of Earth from space. He perfectly described how that view makes us keenly aware that our little planet is just a pale blue dot floating in an immensity of space, and our only home, where we and everyone we love, and everyone who has ever lived, has spent their lives. And he pointed out that recognizing that all of humanity's creation, and millennia of delight and pain, of hubris and striving, have taken place on this tiny, distant speck must surely help us realize the importance of being decent and careful with each other, and of protecting and loving the Earth.

If only we could immediately send all members of our governing bodies, politicians and judges and thinkers, into outer space—and allow them to eventually return—to instill in them the urgency of protecting our planet.

You don't have to leave this blue dot to experience awe, wonder, and the like, but the accounts of mystified astronauts remind us of the importance of being alive to these emotions, to open every door, window, threshold, and portal to their possibility in the world around us.

CHAPTER 4

Nature Deficit Disorder:
On Biophilia

People from a planet without flowers would think we must be mad with joy the whole time to have such things about us.

—IRIS MURDOCH, *A FAIRLY HONOURABLE DEFEAT*

We are joined to the Earth in ways we barely understand. In 1984, American biologist E. O. Wilson coined the term "biophilia" for an innate love of the natural world, which he argued is intrinsic to being human. German social psychologist Erich Fromm called it "the passionate love of life and all that is alive." Wilson suggested that this "innate emotional affiliation of human beings with other living organisms" has a genetic basis, and is found in genetic memories. Scientists have been trying to understand and test the idea ever since. Whatever the basis, the deep craving humans have for nature cannot be denied.

. . .

Theodore Roosevelt understood the pull of the wild the moment the shortsighted boy was given a pair of glasses at the age of twelve. He had always loved nature, and now he began to closely track its inhabitants, especially birds. As a child living in New York, he collected the skull of a seal, birds' nests, mouse skeletons, and insects; he even mounted a snowy owl, which can now be seen in the superb American Museum of Natural History on the west side of Central Park. He especially loved birds, and filled notebooks with diagrams, drawings, and data about various creatures. Yet for all his accumulation of knowledge, he found it difficult to describe the joy of the natural world, writing in 1910: "There are no words that can tell the hidden spirit of the wilderness, that can reveal its mystery, its melancholy, and its charm."

It is fortunate for current generations of Americans that Roosevelt became president of the United States in 1901. Over his life, he ensured that more than 234 million hectares of wilderness would be preserved, in national parks and monuments: Yosemite, the Grand Canyon, Pelican Island. Conservation, to Roosevelt, was an inherently masculine pursuit, like camping and hunting, not something to be defined as left, urban, and "green," as much environmentalism is today. As Jonathan Rosen described it in *The New York Times*, conservation "went with being manly, brave, patriotic. It was as populated with animals as any children's book. It was scientific and yet saturated with religious meaning, patrician but populist, global and yet fueled by jingoistic fervor. It was fun."

But today, Florence Williams, author of the bestselling book *The Nature Fix: Why Nature Makes Us Happier, Healthier, and More Creative*, says we have lost more than we realized, because of our current "epidemic dislocation from the outdoors."

"Yes, we're busy," she writes. "We've got responsibilities. But beyond that, we're experiencing a mass generational amnesia enabled by urbanization and digital creep." And there is an ugly anger marbling public debate now, fueled by the fact that we are crowding together in an increasingly lonely fashion: unable to fully concentrate on faces opposite us, stooping on sidewalks to peer at lit screens, returning home to lament, rage, or throw rotten vegetables online at strangers we may have nodded at on the subway just a few hours earlier.

As Johann Hari writes in *Lost Connections: Uncovering the Real Causes of Depression—and the Unexpected Solutions*, it is only in the past fifteen years that the psychological effects of being cut off from the natural world have been recognized, a condition dubbed "nature deficit disorder." And it is only now that benefits of immersion in nature are being subject to rigorous testing.

All over the world, scientists have been conducting reams of research to assess the psychological and physical rewards of spending time in nature, with all five senses open and alert. They've sent people on walks through remote forests, parks, stands of conifers, and kiwifruit orchards in summertime; flooded them with the scent of cedarwood in laboratories; blindfolded them and given them sheets of aluminum leaves, then real ones, or authentic pansies, then artificial ones—all while monitoring moods, heart rates, cortisol levels in saliva, glucose levels in blood, hypertension, hemoglobin, sleep quality, and subjects' senses of comfort and relaxation, among other things.

And the findings astounded me.

In short: When we are exposed to sunlight, trees, water, or even just a view of green leaves, we become happier, healthier, and stronger. People living in green spaces have more energy and a stronger sense of purpose, and being able to see green spaces from your home is associated with reduced cravings for alcohol, cigarettes, and harmful foods. The closer we live to nature the better, and even just being surrounded by plants can help. A 2019 study of an impressive ninety thousand people found that residential green space in childhood is associated with lower risk of psychiatric disorders from adolescence into adulthood. Fifteen minutes spent wandering in a city park made male Japanese students feel less stressed; a seventeen-minute walk made a group of men more "comfortable, relaxed, natural, vigorous," and less tired, confused, and anxious. When people move to greener areas, depression lifts. Inhabitants of buildings with more gardens and plants are less aggressive, more disciplined, and, according to a Chicago study of public-housing residents, have better concentration. Moods lighten in parks. Kids exposed to nature perform better in tests.

The science is relatively nascent, the sample sizes are small, and questions remain about the potential tangling of causation and correlation, but the consistency of findings across a variety of places, groupings, approaches, and settings is uncanny. A study of mailroom workers found that those workers who had some daily exposure to sunlight were significantly more productive (by up to 16 percent). An assessment of students found those who lived in dorms with green views had better cognitive function than those who didn't. A study of inmates at the State Prison of Southern Michigan showed that the 50 percent of them whose cells looked onto trees were 24 percent less likely to become physically or mentally ill than those who gazed only at brick walls.

Hospital patients who had a view of trees and bushes also did better while recovering from surgery than those who had views of walls; they asked for half the amount of painkillers and buzzed the nurses half as often. This study, conducted by Roger Ulrich in 1984, prompted many hospitals to plant "healing gardens."

A Canadian study found that having ten or more trees in a city block "improves health perception in a way that is like an increase in annual personal salary of $10,000." Even better, "having eleven more trees in a city block decreased cardio-metabolic conditions in ways compared to an increase in an annual personal income of $20,000." In another study, people leaving an urban park were more likely to help a passerby than those entering it.

As Florence Williams says simply: "The more nature, the better you feel."

...

More than a century ago, Florence Nightingale instinctively understood that plants and gardens had therapeutic properties. In her seminal work *Notes on Nursing,* written in 1859, she outlined her belief that patients would heal better if they were able to look at beauty, brilliant colors, and a variety of objects, or just some kind of view:

> I have seen, in fevers (and felt, when I was a fever patient myself) the most acute suffering produced from the patient (in a hut) not being able to see out of [a] window, and the knots in the wood being the only view. I shall never forget the rapture of fever patients over a bunch of bright-colored flowers. I remember (in my own case) a nosegay of wild flowers being sent me, and from that moment recovery becoming more rapid.
>
> People say the effect is only on the mind. It is no such thing. The effect is on the body too. Little as we know about the way in which we are affected by form, by color and light, we do know this, that they have an actual physical effect.

Unsurprisingly, much of the early pioneering research into the ways in which nature can counter the darker sides of urbanization originated in the world's largest city, Tokyo, which currently houses thirty-seven million people in its greater metropolitan area. In the 1980s, increasing awareness in Japan of the benefits of dousing yourself with nature gave rise to the practice of forest bathing, or *shinrin-yoku*. Based on ancient Buddhist and Shinto practices, forest bathing is a kind of preventative medicine that involves immersing yourself in nature while engaging all the senses; it has recently spread throughout the Western world.

Dr. Qing Li, an environmental immunologist at Tokyo's Nippon Medical School, has led the research into the science, and his book *Shinrin-Yoku: The Art and Science of Forest-Bathing* invites us to immerse ourselves in nature. In 2010, Li found that the number and activity level of immunity-supporting cells rose after a forest visit and stayed elevated for a month; the cells did not respond in any way to carefully crafted similar trips in urban places. Since then, research has also shown that forest bathing has positive benefits on the cardiovascular system, especially in reducing hypertension and coronary artery disease; the respiratory system, including alleviating allergies; and mental health, by reducing depression and anxiety (and even ADHD), enhancing mental relaxation, and increasing feelings of awe, which in turn leads to an increase in gratitude and selflessness. Sitting in his small, uncluttered office in Tokyo, Dr. Li told me that people suffering "nature deficit disorder" regularly come to him seeking a cure for a problem they have no name for: a general unease, anxiety, or sadness—crucially, a forest walk has been shown to limit, or decrease, rumination. His passion is obvious: The science has repeatedly confirmed his gut instinct, and now he is called upon to give lectures around the world on the subject.

Ongoing worldwide research confirms the benefits of bathing in nature. In 2017, a meta-analysis assessed sixty-four studies of forest bathing published between 2007 and 2017. The authors stressed the need for longitudinal research but found strong evidence that time in nature reduces stress, including "technostress." Bathing in nature was found to help Danish soldiers with PTSD; Koreans who have suffered strokes, neck aches, or chronic pain; Swedish dementia patients; Chinese hypertension sufferers; Israeli school students with learning difficulties; Japanese diabetics and cancer patients; stressed Florida office workers; Lithuanians with heart disease; and depressed American retirees.

In one study of Korean patients who had been hospitalized for depression, psychotherapy carried out in a forest had discernibly superior results to the same therapy performed in a hospital. In another study, severe depression in alcoholics was lightened. The health benefits spanned ages—from childhood obesity (a survey of seven thousand children in Indianapolis found a lower incidence of obesity in greener neighborhoods) to longevity in adults (a Tokyo study of three thousand people over seventy-five found mortality was protected by "green, walkable paths and spaces," irrespective of age, sex, marital or socioeconomic status, or initial health). Nature therapy has also significantly decreased the pulses of anxious middle-aged Japanese women and the blood pressure of middle-aged Japanese men, and made both genders sleep more deeply. Just sitting on a chair and looking at a forest made a group of young male students calmer, according to analysis of their saliva.

The authors of the 2017 meta-analysis wrote:

In general, from a physiological perspective, significant empirical research findings point to a reduction in human heart rate and blood pressure and an increase in relaxation for participants exposed to natural green spaces. . . . This in-depth review illustrates, honors, and supports the increased awareness of the positive health-related effects (e.g., stress reduction and increased holistic well-being) associated with humans spending time in nature, viewing nature scenes via video, being exposed to foliage and flowers indoors and the development of urban green spaces in large metropolitan areas worldwide. Not only valid and reliable psychometrics have been implemented, but valid and reliable physiological measurements have been used to show significant and potentially healing and health promoting effects.

They also concluded that the cardiovascular benefits of forest bathing "are apparent regardless of age, gender, socioeconomic background, or previous exposure to a nature setting."

There are some significant shortcomings with the research. Many sample sizes are small; most measure only brief, single exposures to nature; and many subjects are young, healthy male students—more randomized, controlled experiments are needed. The impact of physical activity is not often differentiated, although many studies compare the same levels of activity—mostly walking—in city and forested areas. And the effects studied are short-term: The longevity of benefits has not been determined. There are still many questions, too, about how to define green space, and exactly what kind and length of exposure to nature is required, and whether you need to be in nature or just focus on it. But the findings about mood improvement are unequivocal, and, as Frances E. "Ming" Kuo of the University of Illinois has pointed out, it is natural to assume, according to the evidence so far, that "total exposure is important, all forms and quantities of exposure are helpful; and the greener the better." Especially in the sharpest and harshest of urban environments.

· · ·

About a decade ago, the world scale finally tipped from the country to the city, as urban dwellers began to outweigh country dwellers. Today, about 55 percent of us live in cities: a mind-boggling shift that we seem to have barely grappled with. The United Nations estimates that by the 2050s more than two-thirds of us will inhabit urban areas, and this figure will be much higher in the developed world. For all the unknown consequences, of one thing we can be certain: More and more of us will become deprived or starved of nature; will spend days and months without glimpsing an expanse of green, a stretch of blue, or an uninterrupted horizon; and will surely experience, as a result, a kind of unidentified ache or restlessness.

What will the effect of this be on our psyches? In short, we do not yet fully know, but the early signs are clear, and the evidence is building. Urbanization has already been associated with mental illness, though it is not certain why. Instinctively, many of us are feeling the discomfort of disconnection from nature. We willingly pay for apps that treat us like grounded teenagers by blocking Wi-Fi access; we google "blackspot" resorts that force us to log off and stare at the hills, the trees, or the starry sky as we try to still the habitual twitching of our hands.

...

Our need for nature is something Frederick Law Olmsted understood perfectly, to the great luck of anyone who has ever lived in New York City, another one of the world's largest, shiniest metropolises, bulging with people, dreams, fairy-lit trees, rats, and surprisingly high piles of garbage. In 1865, the brilliant landscape architect, who strongly believed that parks must be available to all, wrote: "It is a scientific fact that the occasional contemplation of natural scenes of an impressive character . . . is favorable to the health and vigor of men." The idea was not actually an established fact then—it was only a guess—but he was right.

Such contemplation, of course, is the entire purpose of Central Park, that haven of green in a dense, crowded city. There, not only kids play; people skate and dance and run and bike and walk dogs and drink and fall in and out of love. I still get a pang sometimes when I think about Central Park; it is that expanse of wood and pond and crag and green that crowns for me the ten years I spent in that city, my second home. I got my first crush in New York, aged seven, on a boy called Alex, who had a blond bowl cut, when my family lived in Rye, a suburb of New York City. I wrote a play there with my friend Erica when I was eight, called *Counterfeiting Petticoats*, about a group of pioneer women who printed money and drove wagons to freedom. I ran away from home there when I was ten; and then, much later, I got engaged there, in a giddy whirl of cocktails, helicopter rides, and walks through the park—then bedecked with orange flags by the artist Christo. I also gave birth to my son in New York, in a hospital dwarfed by a thicket of tall buildings, and worked at a newsmagazine at the southwestern corner of Central Park.

After moving back to Australia, I missed many things: the perfect smoked-salmon bagels; the smell of hot sugar peanuts and roasted chestnuts; the obscene hiss of subway steam; the thickness of the Sunday *New York Times*; the proximity of (and events with) thinkers and authors; the lure of Broadway; the mirrored bars; the red leather booths in restaurants; the dive bars of the East and West Villages. Truman Capote said, "I love New York, even though it isn't mine, the way something has to be, a tree or a street or a house, something, anyway, that belongs to me because I belong to it." I felt the same way. New York doesn't belong to me or any of the thousands of other bug-eyed expats who perch on the city's edge and marvel at the skyline's chutzpah. But, in many ways, I belong to it.

And, most of all, I love Central Park, and will always be grateful to the farsighted Olmsted and his design partner, Calvert Vaux, for the surprising stillness it gave me, as a mother of tiny children with an intense job and a stressed, stretched husband, in the midst of urban-jungle noise, blasting horns, shouting, commercials distorting through cheap speakers, and the constant beeping of traffic crossings. I lived on the Upper West Side, behind a Unitarian church that held blessing services for dogs and cats and faced the park. I walked from West Seventy-sixth to Fifty-ninth to get to work, so every day I wove down through the park, past the stretch of Sheep Meadow and into Columbus Circle. When I began the research for my book on Queen Victoria, I'd walk across the park, past the mossy green Turtle Pond and Belvedere Castle, to the New York Society Library.

Other times, I rode my bike in easy loops, my babies perched in big seats on the back, and walked marathons around the Jacqueline Kennedy Onassis Reservoir with friends, talking in rapid torrents as the water gently rippled. I remember walking from Fifth Avenue and Fiftieth through the park up to Eightieth with a close friend, laughing and swinging big bags containing boots we had bought on sale at Saks, as golden leaves—the first of fall—dropped quietly around us in what seemed to be an enchanted wood. In autumn, I carefully watched the trees turn orange, then red, from my office window—there would always be one to lead, and another to trail, then others. With the branches of winter bare, each side of the park was again exposed to the other: The west could see the east again, with its fancy stores and billionaires' houses that glittered across the quiet expanse.

In Central Park, I sat and nursed my son—a jolly baby who wanted only milk and affection—on benches lining the park's horse-riding tracks. I draped my chest with material to try to ensure no New Yorkers were alarmed—women rarely breastfeed in public there—but I was stared at almost every time. I held my daughter's birthday parties on rugs in lush little dells, where cupcakes tilted precariously on tufts of grass. At one party, she tore her clothes off and rolled in the dirt with a giant inflatable giraffe her fairy godfather had brought from Tribeca on the roof of a cab.

When I lived in Manhattan, I often longed for my children to be able to run barefoot in summer in places other than city parks, not to fry like eggs on dirty, steaming sidewalks in the heat, nor see rats coughing up poison on our street corner, surrounded by mounds of stinking trash, or suffer the round of inexplicable flus that seem to frequently plague kids, particularly in New York City. I wanted them to know a country of endless ocean waves, broad skies, and red dirt. But once we were back in Australia, I also wanted my children to know Christmas in New York, to inhale the scent of pine trees leaning against lampposts, and wander Fifth Avenue with their faces lit by the glowing panther made of lights crawling up the Cartier store, and the rows of trees wrapped with tiny, twinkling globes. I wanted them to press their noses against shop windows, and gasp at the large white Yeti at Saks, the boy wandering through a crystal forest at Macy's, and Santa steering a gondola at Bloomingdale's.

Especially, still, I want them to know snow, the heart-pounding rush of sleds on dirty white hills, the sudden muffled hush of blizzards, the vision of Central Park covered in slippery ice. The most magical moments in the park were in the early morning after it had just snowed and before anyone had been able to grab their sleds, when all was still and achingly pretty, and my footprints were the first to puncture the smooth white. I would take our old chocolate Labrador, Hugo, running with me—he was allowed off his leash before nine A.M., and he bounded about clumsily and happily like a large puppy, jaws snapping at the white powder, leaping into large, crisp drifts.

It is Central Park that I will always think of when I most miss New York. It won't be the astounding convenience of twenty-four-hour availability; the skull-sized chocolate-chip cookies from Levain Bakery; the rooftop bars; the Catherine wheel of creative output in museums, galleries, opera halls, and libraries; the endless reinvention; or the eccentric people with gargantuan brains that will make my heart twinge when I remember that city. Instead it will be the hours I spent running past the icy rowboat lake and up past the wildness of the Ramble, the snow-stacked branches, the sound of my feet hitting icy dirt, and the joy on my dog's face. For me, that New York defies a million other New Yorks, and reminds me how urban some dreams are. In a city of cloud-grazing buildings, Central Park was a rectangular refuge of trees, the place where I was most at peace.

. . .

We all need our own central parks. They may just be back-yards or winding paths or nooks in trees. When I was a kid, one of my special places was Long Island Sound, an estuary full of waterbirds and shorebirds such as piping plovers, os-preys, and little least terns, stretching far behind our house in Rye, New York. Later it was a little patch of rain forest with a running creek next to a muddy football field in Sydney; then the seawater of Gordon's Bay, Clovelly; then Central Park; and finally Cabbage Tree Bay, Manly, in Sydney. If I close my eyes and place myself under the water there, I feel calm.

Studies have found you need to spend only a little over an hour a week in such places to experience a shift in mood, however slight. American professor Wilbert Gesler calls them "therapeutic landscapes" that provide a "healing sense of place." Gesler is a health geographer, someone who seeks to understand the way people interact with the environment, and how places and locations can affect health and well-being.

The widespread acceptance that these benefits are real helps explain why forest bathing has gone from alternative therapy to mainstream practice. Yet no one really knows why it works. It could be the peace, the distraction, the fact that our brains can unfurl, the birdsong, or even chemicals (phytoncides) exuded by trees, as Dr. Li believes. Think of the terms used by nature scientists to describe the way humans act in forests. "Effortless attention." "Soft fascination." "Absorption."

Whatever the case, as environmental scientist Frances Kuo says, "The scientific literature on dosage suggests that nature helps in every form, and in every dose." As a result, today, around the world, in Canada, the United States, Japan, Australia, Korea, Scotland, and England, hundreds of people are training as forest guides, or tree therapists. Once qualified, they take groups of people through woods slowly, encouraging them to take in their surroundings with every sense. There are programs for cancer patients, disadvantaged children, unwell teenagers, veterans with PTSD. Everywhere, curious souls are closing their eyes in woods, listening to birdsong and rustling leaves, smelling moss, oaks, eucalypts, ferns, flowers in bloom, and breathing deeply, hoping to find something they feel they have lost—or, at the very least, to sense it nearby.

· · ·

It took me decades to work this out. I used to see camping as earnest and laborious and too much work. I went to scout camp when I was about fourteen and hated it. It rained, and one of the pimply scouts kept trying to pin me up against trees when we were doing chores, and the toilet paper ran out, and I thought I was in hell. It has taken me many years to realize that those skills of navigating the natural world, of diving, hiking, and paddling, aren't just about collecting badges on a scout's uniform: Along with our flashlights and thick-soled boots, they are tools for hunting and experiencing awe and wonder. In the years I spent backpacking around Europe and Asia, after late nights spent dancing and exploring local bars, I used to jam a pillow over my head when sleeping at youth hostels to block out the sounds of those mainly Northern European travelers who would set their alarms, rise early, put on their sensible clothes and hiking boots, then loudly crunch muesli while examining maps of the day's hike. I should have gone with them.

It wasn't until I was in my midtwenties that I began to go trekking and river rafting whenever I could—first in the Himalayas of Nepal, then the Atlas Mountains in Morocco. When I think of my own experiences of joy, I think of sitting, suntanned and dirty, on top of a rickety bus, hurtling along narrow roads on a mountainside in Nepal after a two-week rafting trip, my legs jammed under luggage ropes to ensure I wouldn't fall off when we swerved around cliff edges. I was singing the Carpenters' "Top of the World" at the top of my voice and grinning at my friends when I suddenly realized it would not be possible to feel happier, or more free.

· · ·

It's not just forests that uplift us, but oceans, too. A 2010 multi-study analysis found just five minutes spent at the coast was enough to strengthen us. It also found, to the surprise of precisely no one in my swim group, that while "every green environment improved both self-esteem and mood, the presence of water generated greater effects." Even better than the forests!

Water even buoys us when we are not in it. A 2016 study from Michigan State University and the University of Canterbury in New Zealand found that in Wellington "higher levels of blue space visibility were associated with lower psychological distress." This is true for me every day I swim.

Sometimes I wonder if sunbathing is similar to forest bathing. Not sunbathing in the sense of frying in oil, or bikini-basting on a beach like a lamb on a rotisserie spit, but just sitting in the warm sun, or lying on rocks like a basking seal, drying out after a cold swim. The greatest obsolete word, which I am eager to bring back into usage, is "apricity," meaning "the warmth of the winter sun." When you've plunged into icy seas and returned to shore with stiff red fingers and numb toes, there can be few delights as sweet as sitting in the sun's light, soaking up the apricity, thawing down to the bone. Doris Lessing once wrote, "All sanity depends on this: that it should be a delight to feel the roughness of a carpet under smooth soles, a delight to feel heat strike the skin, a delight to stand upright, knowing the bones are moving easily under flesh."

In my view the simplest explanation for our intense connection with nature, our biophilia, remains the most plausible: We hanker for the sight of green and blue, for the Earth of our ancestors, the sea of our origins, and the feeling on our faces of the sunlight that first nurtured life. We sense this instinctively—it's in our wiring, which makes it even more confounding when we choose to ignore it, and allow vast tracts of wilderness to vanish or burn, noise to creep across once-silent hills, plastics to choke oceans, and years to pass without pausing as we did when we were children, and stare up through the branches.

· · ·

Indigenous people have known all these things for millennia. Appreciation of the benefits of nature is an ancient wisdom that most people are only barely beginning to comprehend, or regain, as the Earth heats, ice melts, and species vanish. Australian Aboriginal and Torres Strait Islander people belong to the world's oldest continuous living culture. A connection to country is a fundamental part of their identity and of understanding their ancestors and their stories, in which everything that lives is entwined with and linked to every other living thing.

In these traditions, then, people are the custodians and caretakers of the land that sustains them. "For Aboriginal peoples," says Palyku woman Ambelin Kwaymullina, "country is much more than a place. Rock, tree, river, hill, animal, human—all were formed of the same substance by the Ancestors who continue to live in land, water, sky. . . . Country is loved, needed and cared for, and country loves, needs and cares for her peoples in turn. Country is family, culture, identity. Country is self." Not only that, but country is the source of life and light. As Kwaymullina says, "In the learning borne of country is the light that nourishes the world."

CHAPTER 5

Why We Need Silence

Let tiny drops of stillness fall gently through my day.
—MIRIAM-ROSE UNGUNMERR-BAUMANN

If I imagine hell as a physical place, of torture and pain, it's not the heat that troubles me most; it's the noise. Hell surely means living in the unceasing din of a construction zone with no time limits, where earplugs and noise-canceling headphones are banned. In the Middle Ages, Christian scholars believed noise was used as a weapon by Satan, who was bent on preventing human beings from being alone with God, or fully with one another, alert and listening. The fictional devil in *The Screwtape Letters*, by C. S. Lewis, detests both music and silence. Hell, he crows, is filled with furious noise, "the audible expression of all that is exultant, ruthless and virile. . . . We will make the whole universe a noise. . . . We have already made great strides in

this direction as regards the Earth. The melodies and si-
lences of Heaven will be shouted down in the end."

Sometimes it seems we're already there. "The day will
come," said Nobel Prize–winning bacteriologist Robert
Koch in 1905, "when man will have to fight noise as inexo-
rably as cholera and the plague." British author Sara Maitland stands ready. She believes the mobile phone was a
"major breakthrough for the powers of hell." Maitland is
more conscious of noise than most—she spent more than
a decade pursuing silence like a hunter chasing its prey. In
A Book of Silence, she describes how she traveled to the
desert, the hills, and the remote Scottish Highlands trying
to discover what silence truly was, and immerse herself in
it. "I am convinced that as a whole society we are losing
something precious in our increasingly silence-avoiding
culture," she writes, "and that somehow, whatever this silence might be, it needs holding, nourishing and unpack-
ing."

After spending forty days in silence in an isolated house
on a windy moor, Maitland found that her physical sensa-
tions were heightened (she was overwhelmed by the deli-
ciousness of porridge, heard different notes in the wind, was
more sensitive to temperature, and more emotional); she
became what she calls "disinhibited" (a Jungian notion that
once alone you are free to do what you want—pick your
nose while eating, strip your clothes off, abandon grooming,
wash infrequently); and she heard voices (a young girl, then
a male choir singing in Latin, which she thinks may have

been the wind). She also experienced great happiness, felt connected with the cosmos, was exhilarated by the risk and peril in what she was doing, and discovered a fierce joy, or bliss.

Maitland rails against the idea of silence as void, absence, and lack—something that we must rush to fill—insisting it is positive and nurturing, and something more profound that should be actively sought. (When silence is imposed, of course, it is something entirely different.)

It's well established that unwanted noise is bad for our health, which is why hospital engineers, architects, and staff are constantly urged to find ways to keep the ward hubbub, and the high-decibel sounds of tech equipment and corridor clatter, low. As Florence Nightingale wrote back in 1859, "Unnecessary noise, then, is the most cruel absence of care which can be inflicted either on the sick or well."

• • •

Silence is not just the absence of noise, or even unnecessary noise. It is the absence of noise made by human beings. Silence is rare, and shrinking. American acoustic ecologist Gordon Hempton, the man known as "the Sound Tracker," defines it as the complete lack of "all audible mechanical vibrations," which leaves "only the sounds of nature at her most natural." True quiet, he says, is the "think tank of the soul."

The real joy of silence is not about blocking out the noise, but reconnecting with, or listening to, the land. This wisdom is a place where hippies, scientists, Indigenous people, wilderness lovers, and the rest of us motley crew can meet. When I was living in New York, I interviewed Hempton, who then had circled the Earth three times recording sound on every continent except Antarctica and had become increasingly disturbed by the disappearance of silence from even the most remote places. He has walked through the Australian outback and the Kalahari Desert, along the edges of volcanoes and deep into forests to track sound. For him, the Earth is a "solar-powered jukebox."

Hempton's conversion to studying sound came one night when, as a twenty-seven-year-old botany student, he slept in a cornfield for a night. He heard crickets, then rolling thunder, then stayed still, listening, as a storm passed over him. He was drenched but delirious, wondering, "How could I be twenty-seven years old and never have truly listened before?" From then on, he carried a microphone and tape recorder with him everywhere, "obsessively listening—freight trains, hobos—it was a flood of sensation."

Now Hempton's passion is the preservation of true natural silence, which he describes not as the "absence of something, but the presence of everything." It is many sounds, he says:

Silence is the moonlit song of the coyote signing the air, and the answer of its mate. It is the falling whisper of snow that will later melt with an astonishing reggae rhythm so crisp that you will want to dance to it. It is the sound of pollinating winged insects vibrating soft tunes as they defensively dart in and out of the pine boughs to temporarily escape the breeze, a mix of insect hum and pine sigh that will stick with you all day. Silence is the passing flock of chestnut-backed chickadees and red-breasted nuthatches, chirping and fluttering, reminding you of your own curiosity.

Today, Hempton says, we are being deprived of an essential need that our distant ancestors had met—to be in the sounds of nature. Even our national parks, he says, are being flooded with noise pollution, especially by overhead aircraft. He describes silence as a marvel.

"Besides spending time away from the damaging noise impacts present at our workplace, neighborhoods, and homes," he told me, "we are given the opportunity not only to heal but discover something incredible—the presence of life, interwoven! Do you know what it sounds like to listen for twenty miles in every direction? That is more than one thousand square miles. When I listen to a naturally silent place and hear nature at its most natural, it is no longer merely sound; it is music. And like all music, good or bad, it affects us deeply. . . . In evolution, earlids never developed, but eyelids did. And to those who know that true listening is worship, silence is one of nature's most transformative sermons. I am filled with gratitude to have heard it."

. . .

What's interesting to me about silence is not just the extremism, often verging on madness, of those who can claim to have truly lived or worked silently: the Arctic explorer, the deep-sea diver, the sailor, the hermit, the ascetic, the nun. What is also important is what the rest of us can wring from the more mundane moments of stillness. We won't all skip nude through the Scottish bracken, or inhabit caves in Tibetan mountains, but we can experience silence in ways so potent they become addictive: the uninterrupted hush after midnight; the sweet intimacy between a mother and her nursing baby in the wee hours; the breathless stillness after excellent sex; the calm of meditation; the loosening of muscles during the Savasana pose in yoga; the hush of awe while gazing at a proud, ancient mountain or soaring down the green tunnel of a wave. Even if it is not pure silence, it can be enough.

The idea of quietly staring at a rock, at piles of sand, or at blinking stars for hours, if not weeks, seems, weirdly, profoundly countercultural today, in a world where people tweet bubbles, livestream the arching of eyebrows, and spend holidays distracted by how best to market themselves on Instagram #goals #bestlife. Are we even capable of being still without our hands darting for our phones? Yet if generations of mystics and seekers have insisted that something connects silence with the sublime, you have to wonder who we could be if we paused more often.

. . .

Just like the need for country, the need to pause is not a modern discovery but an ancient truth. Indigenous Australians, inheritors of the world's oldest living culture, have long known that sometimes, in order to learn, you need to slow down, shut up, and allow yourself to sit in silence. Which is exactly what my TV crew and I were told to do when we entered the sacred ceremonial grounds at Gulkula in North East Arnhem Land in the Northern Territory of Australia, the home of the Yolngu clan.

While speeding along the red dirt road to the campsite for the Garma Festival of Traditional Cultures in 2018, I carefully read the "behavior protocols" provided by the Yothu Yindi Foundation. They state: "Remember you are on Yolngu land and entering Yolngu time. Yolngu perceptions, priorities, and preoccupations are different from those of mainstream Australia. Be patient, and try to leave at home your expectations of how things are learned, and how events should run. Traditionally, Yolngu learn by observation, by looking and listening. Asking too many questions can be inappropriate. So when you have questions, choose them carefully and thoughtfully."

Winnowing questions can be a challenge for a journalist. But doing just that, sitting back with my eyes open and ears cocked, resulted in one of the most intense experiences of my life, a shift and a shake of the kaleidoscope. It was an enormous privilege to be briefly immersed in this ancient, calm, respectful tradition, during the country's largest gathering of Indigenous elders, where truth telling was the theme, and to recognize the lived, enduring shame of the treatment of Indigenous Australians as well as the depth of their spiritual and cultural traditions. These myriad, dynamic, and compelling traditions should be a source of immense pride to Australians, just as the Maori culture is to New Zealanders; the atavistic wisdom contained in these cultures connects us to our land in ways we still barely fathom, and has done so for more than sixty-five thousand years.

Aboriginal people have long spoken of the need to listen to country. At a time when we are addicted to screens, filter our own faces in selfies, exercise on machines, and talk to robots, wondering why there is so much anxiety and depression, can there be any more potent call than to slow, forget ourselves, sit under trees and stars, and listen to country and to those who inherited it from their ancestors?

On our last morning at Garma we went to a sacred women's crying ceremony held at 5:30 A.M. as the sky lightened from black. Female Aboriginal elders—the matriarchs—cried for their land and their people, mourned and comforted and called to one another. We sat in silence, ringed by smoldering fires and eucalypts on a ridge with views of the far-off sea, transfixed. It was suffering and solace in song, a lament of love, a raw paean to life. It was unlike anything I have ever heard. And, at the end, the women paused and one of the elders (who gave me permission to write this) said: "And now we wait for the bird to sing." One minute later, it did.

Now, said the elder, "You have been welcomed by the old ladies"—the greatest of honors. The Garma protocols say: "Treat old people with the greatest of respect—they hold the knowledge and the power." It was understood that we would respect the wisdom of these women, who create and sustain life. I went home and told my kids—to their mirth—that being welcomed by the "old ladies" really meant "bow down to your queens."

One of those old ladies is the remarkable Miriam-Rose Ungunmerr-Baumann, a Christian Indigenous elder from the Nauiyu community of the Daly River in the Northern Territory, who believes that the greatest gift her people can give to fellow Australians is a respect for silence and alert, calm contemplation. This is called many different names in different Indigenous languages across Australia, but in her Ngangikurungkurr language it is known as *dadirri* and means, specifically, "inner, deep listening and quiet, still awareness."

"Everyone's got it," she says. "It's just that they haven't [all] found it."

In a reflection, Miriam-Rose explains:

Dadirri recognizes the deep spring that is inside us. We call on it and it calls to us. . . . It is something like what you call "contemplation."

When I experience *dadirri*, I am made whole

again. I can sit on the riverbank or walk through the trees; even if someone close to me has passed away, I can find my peace in this silent awareness. There is no need of words. A big part of *dadirri* is listening. Through the years, we have listened to our stories. They are told and sung, over and over, as the seasons go by. Today we still gather around the campfires and together we hear the sacred stories.

The contemplative way of *dadirri* spreads over our whole life. It renews us and brings us peace. It makes us feel whole again. . . .

In our Aboriginal way, we learned to listen from our earliest days. We learned by watching and listening, waiting and then acting. . . . There is no need to reflect too much and to do a lot of thinking. It is just being aware.

My people are not threatened by silence. They are completely at home in it. They have lived for thousands of years with Nature's quietness. My people today recognize and experience in this quietness the great Life-giving Spirit, the Father of us all. It is easy for me to experience God's presence. When I am out hunting, when I am in the bush, among the trees, on a hill or by a billabong; these are the times when I can simply be in God's presence. . . .

Our Aboriginal culture has taught us to be still and to wait. We do not try to hurry things up. We let them follow their natural course—like the seasons. We watch the moon in each of its phases. We wait for the rain to fill our rivers and water the thirsty earth. . . . When twilight comes, we prepare for the night. At dawn we rise with the sun.

We don't like to hurry. There is nothing more important than what we are attending to. There is nothing more urgent that we must hurry away for.

We wait on God, too. His time is the right time. . . .

To be still brings peace — and it brings understanding. When we are really still in the bush, we concentrate. We are aware of the anthills and the turtles and the water lilies. Our culture is different. We are asking our fellow Australians to take time to know us, to be still and to listen to us. . . .

In greeting each morning, remind yourself of *dadirri* by blessing yourself with the following: Let tiny drops of stillness fall gently through my day.

. . .

People like Sara Maitland thrive on gulps and ponds of stillness, large bodies of silent water. She still lives with her dog on the high moorland of Galloway in southwestern Scotland, with no phone.

But what of those of us who aren't hermits?

Sometimes, in the midst of bleeping screens, tiny hands tugging at us with infinite needs, stories to craft, reports to write, emails to hammer out, stomachs to fill, we need to reach for those tiny drops of stillness. And they can fall throughout our day, in snatched or carved-out moments, even in the midst of working, commuting, loving. I often find them, when I dive into water, when I walk the dog, when I stop to sit on a bench and look at the sky, when I sink into my mat at the end of a yoga class, when I curl up with a cup of tea on my porch. I also find them when I sit on the top deck of the ferry that takes me to Sydney's Central Business District, my eyes stinging in the wind, staring at harbor cliffs, tilting sailboats, seagulls gliding in the slipstream. Or just when I lie in bed at night, curling on my side, wondering, and waiting for dream shutters to fall.

PART II

We Are All Wiggly

Why we need to tell our imperfect stories

Sometimes we do not allow ourselves to glow. Instead of looking outward, we stare glumly, or obsessively, at ourselves. We spit at our own reflections in the mirror. We chew on regrets like baseballers on tobacco. We too often tell stories of our own lives that are relentlessly negative—ones of failure, mishap, wasted time, and fruitless work. We talk of our losses, our errors, our flaws, and the unbridgeable gap between some kind of perfection and ourselves. As E. M. Forster wrote, "Actual life is full of false clues and signposts that lead nowhere." Actual life is often incoherent and messy. Actual faces have lumps and bumps and wrinkles. Quite often, actual life really sucks. But then, somehow, it can get better.

Sometimes, when we tell our stories, or create what Northwestern University psychologist Dan McAdams calls a "narrative identity" about ourselves, we recount tales of redemption, of motion, of lessons learned, successes earned.

At other times we tell what McAdams calls a "contamination story," in which our lives inevitably arc from good to bad. An example might be that when we were in primary school we were bullied mercilessly, and that has permanently scarred us. A redemptive story, on the other hand, might be that we were bullied but learned to fight, and made one true friend whose loyalty was unsurpassed. Therapists often look at the crafting of these kinds of stories to reframe a client's thinking and help them understand that events have meaning, and they themselves are not without control or choice. Psychologists have also long found signs that the negative, or pessimistic recounting of our own stories, especially in young adulthood, can increase the risk factor of illness when we are older.

So, what are the stories we tell of our own lives?

In 2013, researchers Dan McAdams and Brady Jones plowed through a stack of adult biographies in search of clues to a fascinating question: Are there any early signs of generativity, or "an adult's commitment to caring for and contributing to the well-being of future generations"? Over a nine-year period, they gathered 158 life stories. The authors found that generative people frequently recounted stories about people who had supported them, and viewed their lives as part of "a network of individuals and institutions that have, over time, provided them with help, opportunities, support and other benefits." (Narcissistic people were less likely to have this view, and more likely to take credit for their own success.) These findings are important because they show that the effects of kindness can flow on for decades, so that generative acts inspire others to act the same way, and "create a virtuous cycle of care, generation after generation." (Financial stability, it should be noted, often also needs to be present for this to occur.)

In *The Man Who Mistook His Wife for a Hat,* Oliver Sacks wrote: "We have, each of us, a life-story, an inner narrative—whose continuity, whose sense, is our lives. It might be said that each of us constructs, and lives, a 'narrative,' and that this narrative is us, our identities. If we wish to know about a man, we ask 'What is his story, his real, inmost story?'—for each of us is a biography, a story."

Why does this matter? Because your story matters. Because too frequently we tell tales of failure and we forget to honor the fact that we tried, the fact that we had purpose, that we cared. I want to talk about the importance of telling your story, even if it is not one that ends in confetti, fanfare, and paparazzi packs. Even if what you have achieved seems to have vanished, seems intangible, or is not recognized, you can recognize it yourself. Part of validating your own story is finding your voice and claiming your authority, especially for the women and introverts among us. And a crucial part of all of this is the need to accept your imperfections, to shrug off lame dictates about how to dress and the need to please, and to stop beating yourself up when you don't feel #blessed or #well and you are really feeling more like #FML or #everythingiscrap.

We all instinctively knew how destructive social media

could be, even before the research confirmed it. There is a reason Madonna recently said Instagram was designed "to make you feel bad." "People are really a slave to winning people's approvals," she told *The Sun*. A recent British survey found that among common social media platforms Instagram had the worst effect on young people's mental health, with one respondent expressing a common lament: "Instagram easily makes girls and women feel as if their bodies aren't good enough as people add filters and edit their pictures in order for them to look 'perfect.'" Now women are asking surgeons for "Instagram faces" that look like they have been filtered. We see so many startled eyes, smooth foreheads, and puffy lips that we have almost forgotten what beauty is—and this matters, because too many of us feel like failures the moment we look in the mirror, before our days have even begun. We need to change our lenses—be gentle with ourselves and harsh with those forces that try to teach us to hate ourselves.

It's never going to be simple, but the best way to bulldoze over the expectation of approval is to master your own story. Sacks wrote: "To be ourselves we must have ourselves—possess, if need be re-possess, our life stories. We must 'recollect' ourselves, recollect the inner drama, the narrative, of ourselves. A man needs such a narrative, a continuous inner narrative, to maintain his identity, his self." A woman, too. As the inordinately wise Eleanor Roosevelt said, no one can make you feel inferior unless you consent to them doing so. She was right—and we need to refuse to give that consent.

CHAPTER 6

The Activist's Attic

In a corner of a lower floor in the Museum of London stand several glass cases that hold relics of the suffragette movement. In the rows of inert objects you can glimpse the force of the protestors' actions, their anger, and their daring: large, broad brown leather belts with thick chains that stretched through dresses to railings, and axes that slashed through paintings and smashed windows. It is these signs of guerrilla combat that are the most striking. The axes are slender, almost delicate. And next to them are memorial brooches featuring axes on backgrounds of flowered material; you can imagine them being pinned to bosoms at meetings—"Nice work at the National Gallery, love." Slash, destroy, pin on a pretty brooch.

Yet what is also significant is what is not displayed in these boxes, not pinned and preserved as emblems of combat: the ephemera of the grinding middle years, the time after the initial excitement of starting a movement and be-

fore the eventual triumph of reform. Absent are the memoranda from the decades before the public eruptions, from
the decades of slog and sweat and boredom; the times of
endless meetings and arguments between the suffragettes
(militant, violent, female-only protesters), suffragists (peaceful campaigners, among whom men were included), and
others who wanted to improve the lot of women, all eventually muddling together and gathering behind the banner of
VOTES FOR WOMEN; the years when it was a battle to get anyone to turn up, when the air was thick with the smoke of
social disapproval, when individual agitation was under-
mined by internal bickering, when the strength of opposition or the glacial pace of change made dissent seem futile,
or when a handful turned up to protest only to find it seemed
like no one cared.

We don't celebrate the boring years of social movements,
only the daring actions and headlines, the eventual victory
and acclaim. We hunt for evidence of the headiness of soli-
darity, not the interminable minutes of, say, a hundred
women's groups, laced with passive aggression and conflict
along with a thirst for change. But the history of women's
liberation has not been just bonnets bobbing behind
banners—remembering that the first official "wave" was
about suffrage for white women—or Indigenous women
like Faith Bandler successfully campaigning for the vote in
the lead-up to the 1967 referendum in Australia, or the brilliant activism of African American women during the civil
rights movement, or an ocean of pink pussyhats (which

were criticized for excluding transgender women and women of color) flooding the streets of Washington, D.C., during the 2017 Women's March, or the lava flow of #MeToo stories after the rapacious film mogul Harvey Weinstein was finally outed as a predator.

It's not just the story of eventual, roaring, undergarment-tearing success, but also the story of a thousand "failures"—of women who continued to speak when no one was listening, bills had been defeated, the numbers were against them, and they'd been told to give up; of women who burned with the fervor of hope for equality only to be dismissed as insane, troubled, hysterical, or angry by their entire neighborhood, family, or community. It's the story of women who kept marching, through the long years of ignorance, in the hope that others might hear their footfalls and join in; who knew that this marching really meant making countless phone calls, or sitting by a printer, photocopier, or even fax machine for a week, or some other dull, repetitive, unglamorous work, or painting signs, or making large pots of tea. None of this was failure—it was persistence—even if it felt like failure to those in the thick of it. It's a feeling I am very familiar with.

...

It is difficult to say exactly why for two decades I kept nine boxes stuffed with clippings, newsletters, minutes, and court transcripts from work I did at university. They traveled from a tiny studio apartment in Sydney's inner city, to musty homes on sea cliffs, into storage for years while I lived in America, and back again to perch on crowded shelves in a little cottage sitting on a peninsula between the harbor and the sea.

They followed me everywhere, these large inchoate cardboard cubes, cracking at the corners and bursting with paper. They were untidy and unresolved. They bothered me; but I could not throw them out. I could not entirely figure out why. I think I wanted to think that the tale they told mattered.

I guess I hoped that one day I would have a story to recount about my twenties, a period lived on inner-city streets and sandy beaches and punctuated by exams, a strange crew of delightful albeit temporary boyfriends, explosive parties, and trips to India. Throughout that time, as I was falling in and out of love, cramming for law exams, and repairing boots when soles wore out on dance floors, I was trying to challenge the Sydney Anglican (Episcopalian, or Church of England) Church's oppression of women, a church I had begun attending with my family when I was ten, and which I have struggled to remain in ever since I began to question their views on women when I was a teenager.

This was a church that still told women to be silent, to not speak of the Bible when men were present, to submit to male authority. A church that tried to rebrand and prettify patriarchy, to pretend it was not ancient but countercultural, resisting the sinful pull of modern feminism. A church many of my friends had fled. For those who stayed, there was comfort and community but often a cost—one uniquely talented friend told me that when she accepted her husband's proposal she had somehow prayed away her sin of ambition.

The boxes dared me to remember.

What is it about a youthful bout of activism that stays with you so long, no matter if you succeed or, in my case, fail spectacularly? Why do we keep these fragments, why do we honor these moments of our younger selves? Is it the memory of hope? Is it the belief that even this history, piecemeal and peripheral, matters? What makes a story worth remembering? Should we collect only remnants of success and sweetness, or also pay homage to foul odors and failure? Is the sweetness simply in the achievement, or more in the striving, and the dreams?

I was a mother of two children in primary school by the time I began going through my boxes. I was tempted to just throw the lot out, but was also conscious of how much of my early self was stuffed in there—all the foolishness and earnestness and taking-myself-seriously. I tried to skip through them quickly, but kept getting snagged on snippets. There is a certain poetry to campaigning for reform: circling an institution, blowing trumpets and occasional raspberries, and demanding to be heard. And what I realized was that here, in my own life, was proof that what we often miss in many sweeping histories of protest—of, say, "waves" of women's protests—is an account of the decades in between, the middle phases of drawn-out campaigns, the years when often all seems futile and lost, and yet people still persist.

That's not just the story of feminism; it's the story of anyone who has sat through PTA or city council meetings, tried to clean up local football fields or stormwater outflows, worked to improve community sport or foster art, or cared about something bigger than themselves, and who found their good intentions led them into a quagmire of boring meetings and years of crushing inaction before things, finally, shifted or changed. It's also the story of those who tried, but never saw anything change, not in their lifetimes. And it's about allowing ourselves to try, and honoring ourselves for caring, striving, and giving a damn.

. . .

It all began, for me, with a court case. In 1992, I was sitting in a law office, paginating documents: stamping them in order, a mind-numbing but vaguely meditative task. I was working as a paralegal to finance my arts/law degree, and had decided to devote a year to writing a history honors thesis, though I was not yet sure of the subject. As I sat there, thumping the pages rhythmically with a stamp, I listened to the radio. During a newsbreak, a woman announced that a bishop was being taken to court because he wanted to allow women to become priests. I dropped the stamp and dashed across the road, up to the courtroom.

The scene was striking. Before me, a row of male judges

faced a row of men in lawyer wigs as a small crowd of women watched from chairs provided for the public. It was a telling image: A group of men from the church were appealing to a group of men of the law to stop women from entering higher ranks. To stop women from speaking for God. To stop women from seeking equality. To stop women.

Something about that smelled bad. In my years of attending local churches I had been told that theology was immutable, ahistorical, and had been engraved on a tablet and passed down by God; and that the only way to interpret Paul's instructions to parts of the early church—that a woman should not have authority over a man—meant that, for all time, women should not be priests. Now I saw this bishop read the Bible another way. I also knew the Bible said not to take fellow believers to court. But now I saw fierce disagreement, and men so desperate to keep women in their place that they were employing the clumsy, expensive instrument of the secular law to do so.

It was a bit rich given that a few years earlier the churches had successfully lobbied for exemptions from the federal anti-discrimination act. They'd wanted to be allowed to discriminate with impunity, to not be bothered by the laws of the land when it came to matters such as employment. And yet now they wanted not to avoid the law, but use it to uphold discrimination.

I returned to my office carrying a press release from the Movement for the Ordination of Women (MOW); I had a topic for my thesis.

...

A few months later, a school friend who went to my church walked up to me at a law ball, just before my date embarrassingly punched another man on the dance floor, and stared at me as I stood holding a glass of red wine. "This research you are doing on women. You know, you are doing the devil's work." I stared back and emptied my glass. I didn't know then how often Christian conservatives had described feminism as demonic, how successfully they had cast female rebellion as sin. The sin, they say, is challenging male authority; to rise up, then, is not answering the call of God but the call of the devil. Women who do this are Jezebels; I have heard stories of women being subjected to exorcism rituals so the spirit of feminism might be cast from them. Even my gentle mother was chastised by Brethren elders for wearing bright lipstick when she was a teenager in the 1950s; she laughed when she told me they called her a Jezebel.

By the time I was at high school, and the national Anglican Church was riven with conflict over whether to make women priests, the stranglehold on women in my conservative hometown of Sydney was tightening. Young girls brimming with hormones were warned not to tempt men with the way we dressed. We were told to marry young and submit to our husbands. We were cautioned against the distraction of social justice, about the evils of ambition, the selfishness of career, the ugliness of feminism. There was a puritanical bent to much of the controlling advice; the need for women to be modest, how just holding hands could be a gateway to sex. I was spoken to once because I had danced for several hours at a party, which was, apparently, evidence of my "love of the pleasures of this world." But the worst thing a woman could be, a friendly leader told me, was opinionated.

Somehow this culture shaped me, then spat me out.

. . .

When I was twenty-three, I joined the synod of the Anglican Diocese of Sydney (the Church of England) to try to persuade the church to allow women to become priests. This was a spectacularly unsuccessful endeavor. The opposition I experienced was cloaked in intense paternalistic politeness. One day, over a lunch break, a priest asked me if I was angry and if he could pray for my anger. That night, a cleric from Sydney's Hills District stood up to argue that we should not waste the time of the synod by even *talking* about women—yet he was trembling from head to toe.

The response from some priests to the suggestion that women's voices be amplified and their roles expanded was peculiarly visceral, enraged, and primitive. One group that opposed women priests, called the Association for Apostolic Ministry, advised members to "avoid contact with irregular female ministers"—essentially, leave the room, walk out of services, or turn your back and flee if such a woman approaches the pulpit.

In 1996, I had a decent run at ramming the church door. I paired up with a judge, Justice Keith Mason, then the solicitor general of New South Wales, and we concocted a halfway solution: that women could be made priests but not heads of parishes. We worked slavishly on submissions, community forums, synod orders, and speeches for many months, all to no avail. We almost won the majority support of the laity (200 for us, 210 against), but the clergy voted solidly against us (151 against, 79 for) and proffered up a petition signed by 1,300 women from conservative churches who said they were perfectly happy with things as they were. Of course they were.

The rub lay here: 87 percent of synod members were men. Two of the three houses that had to pass any motion were made up only of men. This is what is known as a stacked deck: clerical, powerful, with no burden of representation. There were, of course, women who spoke against our bill—all of them married to ministers. They argued that male headship over women was unarguably biblical and meant women could serve only as subordinates.

It was a peculiar, parallel world. Outside the church, and especially among feminist friends, my quest was considered either quaint or uncool; I was told repeatedly to just turn my back on them all, but I was convinced it mattered: The debate about the soul and role of women in the church was one of the deep underpinnings of the cultural objection to, or hostility toward, women exercising any public authority. But at the same time as I was arguing with the patriarchs, I was madly in love with an actor who had four detachable front teeth, my best friend had started dating the woman who was going to be her wife, and I was spending long hours lapping in the sea, playing pool, and dancing with my tribe. I was driven in a way I could not explain to free women from the destructive attitude of the church, but salt water, glitter balls, and the green-capped cliffs of Bondi were my life.

Sadly, all this striving amounted to less than zero: The diocese went backward. After the rest of the Anglican church in Australia and the United Kingdom decided to allow women to be priests in 1992 (this had occurred in the American equivalent, the Episcopalian church, in 1976), the men of Sydney started refusing to allow women in pulpits at all: Indeed, the widely touted rule now is that a woman should not speak if any male past puberty is present (and yes, the idea of policing this is absurd). The doctrine of headship—where a man is to be the head of the woman in the church and home, and she is to submit to him—has been taught more often, and made more rigid. Rendering the church, ultimately, increasingly irrelevant.

. . .

So how to think of these years of effort? Write them off as my wasted youth? Or believe that every effort counts, and that sometimes reform takes a long time? History provides some comfort. British MP William Wilberforce fought against the global slave trade for forty-six years—both inside and outside parliament—until the passage of the Slavery Abolition Act of 1833, which outlawed slavery in most of the British Empire. He died three days after hearing the bill would pass.

Adam Hochschild points out in his book *Bury the Chains* that the beginnings of the Western antislavery campaign can be traced back to the meeting of a dozen Quakers in London in 1787: Eleven of them would be dead before slavery was ended. Wilberforce was the only MP involved, and, as Hochschild argues, it was the first time in history "that a large number of people became outraged, and stayed outraged for many years, over someone *else's* rights." From 1789, Wilberforce began introducing bills in parliament to cease slave trading, but the first time one of them was debated, in 1791, he lost by 163 votes to 88. Then things deteriorated: One report estimated that more than two million whiplashes landed on the bodies of British West Indian slaves every year. Meanwhile, antislavery activists lobbied, drafted petitions, printed pamphlets, and doubtless held thousands of often dull and dispiriting meetings during which they probably wondered if the situation would ever get better and despaired at those who placed financial self-interest and prejudice before the basic right to freedom.

Nelson Mandela spent much of his life, including his twenty-seven years in prison, fighting apartheid before becoming South Africa's first black president, in 1994. Millions of acts of unseen, undocumented dissent and protest had flattened the ground on which he subsequently walked.

Likewise, think of all the scientists who have been warning of the dangers of extreme climate change since the 1960s, and all the criticism of their work and the dismissal of anything resembling agitation or activism as the lunatic alarmism of the left. The public burying of—or attempts to discredit—the crucial findings of thousands of our finest climate scholars will prove to be one of the greatest (if not *the* greatest) acts of political and intellectual corruption of our age.

And what of the Indigenous peoples of Australia seeking constitutional recognition, truth telling, and a voice in parliament—those peoples who have been mistreated, stymied, rejected, ignored, and discriminated against and who continue to ask non-Indigenous Australians to walk with them in a *makarrata*, a Yolngu word meaning "peacemaking," a coming-together after a struggle? The grace of this approach after more than two hundred years of suffering racism, along with their patience, strength, and resilience, is astonishing.

The lesson is: You don't walk away until the work is done.

For every great leader ushering in monumental reform, standing on stages festooned with balloons, blinking in the barrage of flashing camera lights, there are hundreds of thousands of people whose faces we will never see, who have stayed up until midnight painting placards and posters, met with ministers, drafted proposals and policy submissions, marched even when the turnout was dismal, knocked on doors, ignored ridicule, baked cakes, and kept minutes of meetings that seemed to achieve nothing.

Such efforts—when people work for justice or simply to improve the lives of other people, and try to ensure that the voiceless are heard and the marginalized are pulled into the center, but get nowhere for a very long time—are not failures but examples of striving without instant reward. And there is a dignity to this. Sometimes it's enough to have honestly tried—because if we don't try, nothing will ever happen. Walls don't fall at the blast of a single trumpet, nor do tyrants, but only after a long, slow symphony that becomes audible only when it reaches a crescendo.

. . .

Which brings me back to archives. Why do we preserve archives—the stuffed boxes in our attics that tell our own stories, as well as those in distinguished libraries that preserve the documents of influential figures? And where is the line between hoarding and preservation?

What it is crucial to understand is that to keep records is to insist on significance: By doing so, you place something on record, and assert that it is of note. You are saying that it is something people should remember, that they may want to find out about at some point. If it is marked down, they will be able to do that.

Women, historically, have not kept records. They have quilted and stitched. They have scrapbooked, pasted in remnants, sewn fables, and passed stories down through generations, while men have filed official documents. And through these documents, men have dictated the past and determined who we see as winners and losers. This is how power begets power. As Joan M. Schwartz, archival specialist professor of art history at Queen's University Canada, wrote:

> Through archives, the past is controlled. Certain stories are privileged and others marginalized. And archivists are an integral part of this story-telling. In the design of record-keeping systems, in the appraisal and selection of a tiny fragment of all possible records to enter the archive, in approaches to subsequent and ever-changing description and preservation of the archive, and in its patterns of communication and use, archivists continually reshape, reinterpret, and reinvent the archive. This represents enormous power over memory and identity, over the fundamental ways in which society seeks evidence of what its core values are and have been, where it has come from, and where it is going. Archives, then, are not passive storehouses of old stuff, but active sites where social power is negotiated, contested, confirmed.

Historically, archives have excluded the stories of women, of people of color, of the LGBTQIA+ communities, of those inhabiting or pushed to peripheries. The records of their lives have been discarded or lost, while those of small groups of powerful men have been carefully polished, even the smallest fragments collected and kept. Now the rest of us need to insist that our stories matter. Today, thanks to social media, we can, but we must also keep records of these stories. And not just the stories of triumph, victory, or visibility, but of the liminal moments of our lives, and of the long, grinding nature of reform, the bitter, often boring struggle for freedom.

Slash, destroy, pin on a pretty brooch, fade to static.

For me the piles of documents and memoranda in an activist's attic are stories of perseverance. So if you have leaned your weight against something disturbing or unjust and it apparently remained unchanged, remember this: Weight is cumulative. Rebecca Solnit is correct when she argues that "every protest shifts the world's balance" and urges us to remember the "countless acts of resistance on all scales that were never recorded." To reinforce this idea, she employs the metaphor of the mushroom: "The mushrooms that spring up after rain are only the fruiting body of a far larger underground fungus we do not see; the rain causes the mushrooms to rise out of the earth, but the fungus was alive and well (and invisible) beforehand; the rain can be an event."

If we are to tell our stories well, we mustn't limit them to tales of triumph, as though liberation, progress, or success is simply inevitable and inexorable and requires only time—that's a bit like posting only pretty, filtered shots on Instagram. The truth is that progress has always been defined, fueled, and foiled by mess and mistakes as well as might. When you think of your own bursts of activism, or volunteering, or your efforts to just change something you cared about, honor the fact that you tried, whether it was to do with human rights, pipelines, corruption, water, fraud, or freedom. And honor the fact that you stared down defeats and kept going.

This is why we should tell the stories—and value the experiences—of setbacks as well as those of incrementalism and movements; we should talk not just of grenades, shock troops, infantry, masterminds, and strategists but also of stretcher-bearers, bandage makers, and the injured, scarred, deserted, and deeply flawed. The battlefield is vast, and even when the major conflicts have cooled and subsided from public view, someone is always fighting or striving on some patch, somewhere, sending up flares that are very rarely seen. Once they draw the eye, though, they are difficult to ignore.

CHAPTER 7

Honor the Temporary

ephemera

noun 1. something transitory or short-lived 2. (functioning as a plural) a class of collectible items not originally intended to last for more than a short time, such as tickets, posters, postcards, or labels

HISTORY C16: from Greek *ephemeros*: lasting only a day

My son has zero interest in clothes. His dream would be to never have to spend a moment thinking about what to wear, to own garments that would serve for both school and bed. Sometimes he even throws pajamas on top of his school uniform to try to trick me, and to ensure getting dressed in the morning will be a simple, streamlined process. Yet he has somehow amassed a large crate of underpants. I pulled them out recently and pointed out that since he was now ten, we could probably get rid of those sized three and four. He gave me a stern look and said, "But, Mum! Think of all the memories in these underpants!"

I held up one faded pair, with a Pokémon on it. "Oh yeah? What's the memory with this one?"

"We went to the waterslides that time, and it was so great."

"Yeah, it really was, actually," chimed in his sister.

Underpants memories.

But he is right. Objects are memories. What if Marie Kondo's idea about tossing out all objects that don't give us joy makes a crucial omission: that objects have intrinsic value as triggers of memory and nostalgia, and therefore help us document our lives?

And if that's true, which morsels matter, how do we curate the objects in our lives? If I were to hold a museum exhibition called, say, *A Little-Known Baird: The Early Years*, which things would I place behind glass? What would you include in your exhibition? And is this another reason we collect stuff? Because color leaches, memories fade, because the sepia of nostalgia stains mental frames?

Yet why does any of this even matter to us? Perhaps we should stop snapping and gathering, framing and filtering and posting, and learn to accept that there is beauty and depth in temporariness.

. . .

One example of temporary beauty is the mayfly, the insect with the shortest life span on Earth, at just twenty-four hours. (In fact, the adult female of one mayfly species, *Dolania americana*, rarely lives as long as five minutes.) As young nymphs, they can live in the water for several years. But once they become adults, they have only one purpose—to reproduce. Their bellies are filled with air as they float to the water's surface and prepare to become airborne. Quite understandably, they quickly congregate in groups and dance on every surface they can find. Most have just a day or two to dance or to fly.

Cuttlefish live for only a year or two, which still saddens me each spring. *Puya raimondii*, a cactus-like plant known as the Queen of the Andes, does not bloom until it reaches a grand age of between eighty and one hundred years; when it does, it can grow to ten meters tall and produce tens of thousands of flowers along its stem. Other cacti bloom just once a year, for one night. The cherry blossom's glory is also annual, and its shedding is glorious: Petals swirl in eddies in the air, sometimes spiraling to the tops of office buildings— I used to watch the tiny white shapes dance in the wind outside my New York office, high up on the seventeenth floor on West Fifty-seventh Street.

Our attempts to maintain permanence are often clumsy. Pity the poor eighty-one-year-old Spanish widow who tried to restore a two-hundred-year-old *Ecce Homo* (*Behold the Man*) painting by Elías García Martínez, in a sixteenth-century Spanish church in Borja in 2012. She said she was trying to prevent it from being spoiled by damp, but she was ridiculed by the world for turning the face of Jesus into what one critic called "a hairy monkey in an ill-fitting suit." It was quickly dubbed *Ecce Mono* (*Behold the Monkey*)—and is now a tourist attraction. In 2018, in another part of Spain, Estella in Navarre, a local arts and crafts teacher tried to restore a wooden carving of St. George fighting a dragon, but unfortunately transformed it into a cartoonish man resembling Tintin. In mid-2020, experts called for stricter regulation of art restoration after a painting of the Virgin Mary by Spanish painter Bartolomé Esteban Murillo was botched. In truth, restoration is in itself an art form.

But perhaps U.S. author Anne Lamott is right when she says, "Hope and peace have to include acceptance of a certain impermanence to everything, of the certain obliteration of all we love, beauty and light and huge marred love." Some things—and faces—are better left alone. Some things are best left ephemeral.

• • •

Street artists understand the beauty of ephemera because they trade in it. For most of us, the prospect of laboring intensely on murals while perched on ladders, cranes, and cherry pickers for weeks, only to see them subsequently tagged with graffiti or smashed to ruins, is a sobering one. But for street artists, it's a singular thrill. Temporariness is part of the game.

Which on one level is shocking. On another, their attitude resembles the Buddhist view of "attachment," which asserts that clinging to objects, people, or places will only create more suffering for ourselves. Buddha taught that all "conditioned things"—anything that depends on certain conditions for its existence, whether objects, thoughts, or atoms—are impermanent, "by nature arising and passing away." If they arise, he said, and are extinguished, "their eradication brings true happiness." The universal law, then, is that impermanence governs all things. This in some ways echoes the Bible, which repeatedly teaches that attachment to material things, to things of the world, is a distraction, for all must perish.

Street artists practice detachment in a way that can be difficult for an archive-hungry historian like me to fathom; I have spent many years searching for small fragments of evidence, yellowing letters, and water-stained documents in an attempt to understand the past, seeking, above all else, preservation. But not long ago, I found myself standing in an empty old movie theater, the Star Lyric in Melbourne's Fitzroy, looking at an enormous, delicately drawn female face, painted on a wall two stories high, lit by shafts of light from high portholes. It was magnificent. The artist, Rone, knew that developers would destroy the building shortly after his exhibition, *Empty*, closed. A finite life span, he tells me, is what makes street art singular: It blooms suddenly, then is exposed to the elements.

"The temporariness is what makes it contemporary, of the moment, and more important or special," he says. "When someone paints something on the street it won't be protected—anyone can come with spray paint and draw a dick on it, and destroy it—but you walk away, there's not much you can do about it."

Rone, whose full name is Tyrone Wright, is one of Australia's most commercially successful street artists. Dressed in a black cap and T-shirt and a paint-splattered gray hoodie, he shrugs off accusations of being a "sell-out brand" by pointing to the fact that he is delighted that he gets paid to make art, something that would have seemed impossible ten years ago, before the mysterious British artist Banksy (who keeps his or her identity a secret) dragged street art into the mainstream.

Now internationally renowned, Rone has exhibited around the globe, including in London, New York, San Francisco, and Miami, and has painted murals in Taiwan, Malaysia, the United Kingdom, France, New Zealand, Jamaica, the Dominican Republic, the United States, Germany, Japan, and Mexico. His exhibitions—usually photographs of his street art before demolition—sell out to eager collectors before they open.

Next to his desk in the warehouse space he shares with a collective of other artists—who wander around in paint-splattered boiler suits—is an old metal fan, its plastic center melted into long loops, a keepsake from a burned-out house.

He turns to his computer. "Wait, I just wrote this down: 'Beautiful works in places of neglect to highlight what we may have lost.'"

Rone first became known for his portraits of "Jane Doe"—an unknown, unidentified female—which he began painting in 2004 in response to a friend who was painting "screaming vampire faces." He wanted to do the opposite, a "non-aggressive, non-sexual, beautiful image of an unknown woman. I fell in love with the way it worked on the streets—it would decay or fall away—just the eyes would be left, but still beautiful. Nothing lasts forever; it doesn't matter how beautiful it is."

What he speaks of is a fragility meant to heighten appreciation. Rone told me recently, "If you are lucky enough to come across a piece of work you like, you know it may not be there next time you visit, so you have to appreciate it in that moment."

A few days after I met Rone, the Star Lyric was rubble.

. . .

I still maintain that underpants that no longer fit are best thrown out. I do understand the desire to hold on to the memories they might contain, whether magnificent or mundane. But if we are conscious of the temporariness of anything, or everything, we will be far less likely to squander time looking backward, or forward, to moments other than the one we are in.

If we accept that flowering is by its nature a fleeting occurrence, then we are more likely to recognize each bud as a victory, each blossom as a triumph. And if we accept impermanence, we are far more likely to live in the present, to relish the beauty in front of us and the almost infinite possibilities contained in every hour—or a single breath.

CHAPTER 8

Accept Imperfection

When you look at the clouds they are not symmetrical. They do not form fours and they do not come along in cubes, but you know at once that they are not a mess. . . . They are wiggly but, in a way, orderly, although it is difficult for us to describe that kind of order. Now, take a look at yourselves. You are all wiggly. . . . We are just like clouds, rocks and stars. Look at the way the stars are arranged. Do you criticize the way the stars are arranged?

—ALAN W. WATTS, *THE TAO OF PHILOSOPHY*

One of the hardest parts of being a mother of young girls is this: How do you stop them from frowning at their reflection? How do you protect them from the feelings of inadequacy and self-loathing that girls in particular seem to absorb as they grow? How do you teach them to recognize the beauty of a whole person, and not divide themselves into limbs, eyes, noses, breasts—segments that they might decide need "fixing"?

Zadie Smith captured this dilemma well in her 2005 novel *On Beauty*. Her character Kiki Belsey had dreaded having daughters because she worried she wouldn't be able to protect them from self-disgust. Once she had girls, she tried banning television and kept makeup and women's magazines out of her home, but nothing made a jot of difference. Kiki thought that a hatred of women, and of female bodies, was "in the air," and that it was unstoppable, creeping under cracks, coming home on the soles of shoes and inside newspapers. She was unable to stem or control it. And so it was that Kiki thought about this endless self-criticism as she watched her daughter tug at a man's nightshirt she was wearing and say forlornly that she knew that she didn't look "fine."

Some physical flaws are apparent from birth. Others are pointed out to you. I never realized that I had a big nose, for example, until my brother joked about it once at dinner. A short time later, an artist who specialized in caricatures was asked to draw a cartoon of me to run with my newspaper columns. In it, my nose curved so far around my cheek that it almost tickled my ear. I can still remember the roaring laughter of my editor when she saw it. I hated it.

A few days after it appeared, I bumped into the artist—a lovely bloke—in the lift well of our offices, and he asked me what I made of my likeness. I stared at the floor and mumbled. He said, in an awkwardly leading manner, "I really like doing people I work with, as I can capture them so well." There was a pause before he added: "You don't need to have plastic surgery or anything." Oh.

Since then, I have no longer been surprised when random strangers comment on my nose. I once walked into a kebab shop and the proprietor greeted me with: "Aah, you have a French nose! Ha! What would you like to eat?" (By French, I understood she meant more Gérard Depardieu than Emmanuelle Béart.)

My nose is not monstrous, but it would not last a week in Hollywood. Should I care? Sometimes I do, and if it was made of Play-Doh instead of bone and gristle, I admit I'd try to push it in a little, on the sly. I know, we are all "before" shots now, even the conventionally beautiful, and it's increasingly rare to see the face of a prominent person that is untouched. You only have to walk into the changing room of any gym, pool, or surf club and you can view the human body in all its resplendent ordinariness, the kind you will very rarely see onscreen.

It's as though aging is a little . . . embarrassing, unkempt, and sloppy. We shame women, especially as they grow older, tabloids zooming in mercilessly on veined hands or knobbly feet. But we also shame them when they too obviously try not to age. When fillers are too fresh or lips too puffy, when faces look bland and temples tight, we throw pellets of scorn—at women like Renée Zellweger, Kim Novak, Liza Minnelli, and Donatella Versace.

Of course, many prominent women have pricked and in-flated and tortured their faces precisely because of the afore-mentioned criticism of women who show their age. That's what happens when you inhabit a galaxy where wrinkles are a sign not of maturity, but of carelessness and lack of money. It's as though women must both be perfect and mask any striving to that perfection—any sign of straining, or of work, incites contempt.

A vast crowd of people claiming to be surgical Rumpel-stiltskins now skim wealth from women's insecurity like fat off broth, while offering little more than homogeneity. In-deed, it's not surgery that is the problem for the famous faces we gaze upon now, but sameness: the centripetal force that eliminates all "irregularities," all signs of distinctiveness, re-sulting in uniformly stretched eyes, plumped-up cheeks, ironed foreheads, and fully baked breasts. Just ask Jennifer Grey, the *Dirty Dancing* star who lost her distinctive appeal and her career when surgeons shaved her nose down to a more conventional shape.

Perhaps it is time for all of us to trumpet—or at least not try to mask—our imperfections. History is replete with hugely inspiring people who would never have been asked to prance along a Victoria's Secret runway, and wouldn't have wanted to. Think of some of the women! The magnifi-cent Eleanor Roosevelt had buck teeth. The brilliant social worker and campaigner for women's rights Jane Addams thought she had a "lumpy" nose. Mexican artist Frida Kahlo had a unibrow and a mustache. The famed U.S. documentary photographer Dorothea Lange had a limp. Pioneering U.S. chef Julia Child was an impressive six feet two inches tall. So was Margaret Whitlam, wife of the former Australian prime minister Gough Whitlam. She was always self-conscious about her height, and told the Australian Broadcasting Corporation, "I thought of it as being unfortunately too tall. . . . I suppose I was about thirteen; I can remember a picture of myself in my going-skiing gear—and I do look like three yards of pump-water." The writer Daphne Merkin described the fabulously stylish doyenne of postwar fashion Diana Vreeland as having the "face of a gargoyle."

Then there were the monarchs. Egyptian ruler Cleopatra had a hooked nose (French scientist and philosopher Blaise Pascal wrote that if her nose had been shorter, "the whole face of the world would have been changed"). Catherine the Great looked—as recently claimed—like Britain's former prime minister David Cameron in a white wig, yet her perceived plainness did not prevent her from procuring a line of youthful lovers.

Male figures from history can inspire in the same way. Former U.S. president Abraham Lincoln, who was widely considered to be an unattractive man, charmed people with his lack of vanity and pretension. His law partner wrote: "He was not a pretty man by any means, nor was he an ugly one; he was a homely man, careless of his looks, plain-looking and plain-acting. He had no pomp, display, or dignity, so-called. He was a sad-looking man. . . . His apparent gloom impressed his friends, and created sympathy for him—one means of his great success. He was gloomy, abstracted and joyous." He also achieved remarkable things.

. . .

A consequence of uniformity for women—and, increasingly, men—is erasure of character. It seems trite, or retro, to remind ourselves that beauty is warmth, conversation, intelligence, and a certain grace or magnetism, too, but it's true.

Part of the difficulty is that we see allure as simply static, something that can be captured and shared on a flat surface. Our social media imprints have narrowed the definition of beauty to what can be photographed, filtered, and posted; and that has resulted in the neglect of charm.

Charm is often absent from selfies, portraits, and even statues. When, in 1919, the editors of the *Arts Gazette* ran a competition to pick the ugliest statue in London, writer George Bernard Shaw proposed several of Queen Victoria while arguing that these unflattering, stout, solemn figures did her a great disservice. He wondered what crime the by then deceased monarch had committed that she should be so "horribly" portrayed "through the length and breadth of her dominions." He lamented that, although Victoria had been "a little woman with great decision of manner and a beautiful speaking voice which she used in public extremely well" and "carried herself very well," "all young people now believe that she was a huge heap of a woman."

Cleopatra's true allure was her charisma. Plutarch wrote that her beauty was "not in itself so remarkable that none could be compared with her, or that no one could see her without being struck by it." Instead, "the contact of her presence, if you lived with her, was irresistible; the attraction of her person, joining with the charm of her conversation, and the character that attended all she said or did, was something bewitching." Who cared, then, about her nose?

Australian author Elizabeth Jolley described female anxiety about appearance perfectly in her novel *The Orchard Thieves*. She wrote of a grandmother watching a group of young women prepare for a party, wondering why women only ever concentrated on isolated flaws, never "the whole person, the general effect of the complete person." Women only ever saw themselves in flawed fragments, she wrote.

> They were always conscious of the physical fault, the extra chin, the wry mouth, eyes too small or too close together, a flat nose, an ugly nose, fat legs or legs which were too thin and had no shape, lifeless drab hair, the list could go on, and they never, these women, they never saw serenity in their own expressions because of the anxiety reflected in the last-minute glancings in mirrors. The eyes they saw were forever worried and accompanied by small but deep frowns. . . . And, in any case, it was not the physical

details or the clothes and the accessories which mattered most. It was the personality which made the difference between being badly dressed and well dressed.

The red carpet is a cruel carnival. When camera lenses
capture the merest of shadows, the photos are quickly par-
celed into timelines of decay that shout a cautionary message: If you cannot be, and remain, visually pleasing, then
hide. But surely there are enough of us who recognize that
we are more than the sum of our fragmented parts. After all,
superficial beauty is a poor prophylactic against the ills of
the world. The sublime Academy Award–winning actor
Halle Berry told a group of reporters in London in 2004,
when she was promoting *Catwoman*: "Being thought of as a
beautiful woman has spared me nothing in life. No heartache, no trouble. Love has been difficult. Beauty is essentially meaningless, and it's always transitory."

· · ·

Then there's the question: Why do we have to be physically
pleasing at all? I realize it sounds naïve, but can't we just be
good at our jobs, or great company, or simply decent people? Do the biographers of, say, William Gladstone, George
Washington, and King George IV find themselves defend-
ing their subjects against charges of ugliness, as I did when
writing about Queen Victoria, or strain for ways to say that,
at a certain time and in a certain light, they were rather ap-

pealing, actually, or had a "certain beauty"? No, they were usually too absorbed detailing the power and achievements of their men.

Hatshepsut, the pharaoh of Egypt in the fifteenth century B.C., was obese when she died, and had rotten teeth. She was partly bald—the front of her head was bare, but she grew the hair at the back of her head long. Aside from the black and red nail polish she was fond of, she dressed like a male pharaoh, and wore a fake beard. Meredith Small, an anthropologist at Cornell University, described her as looking "like an aging female Dead Head with alopecia." Yet she oversaw Egypt for twenty-two years and was responsible for a remarkable period of prosperity. Her power was greater than any other woman's had been: She acquired the full authority of a male pharaoh, as well as the regalia. Early in her reign she wore flattering, close-fitting gowns and was rumored to have seduced several cabinet ministers. Like Queen Victoria, Hatshepsut seemed to be the kind of person who is more interested in what she thinks of you than what you think of her.

...

The Japanese philosophy of *wabi sabi* perhaps best encapsulates the need to embrace imperfection and transience. As Andrew Juniper has written, *wabi sabi* "is an understated beauty that exists in the modest, rustic, imperfect, or even decayed, an aesthetic sensibility that finds a melancholic beauty in the impermanence of all things."

My talented friend Damien, an art director of films and a photographer, spent months traveling around Japan recording the decay and melancholy in small towns in rural areas—towns emptied of people, with shuttered shops, vacant schools, and deserted streets. He points out that *wabi sabi* is not just an aesthetic but an emotion or outlook, "valuing the old and imperfect and enduring in a world that hankers for the new." In the guide to an exhibition of his works entitled *Wabi Sabi*, Damien quotes Junichiro Tanizaki's 1933 essay on Japanese aesthetics, "In Praise of Shadows," which explained the concept: "We do prefer a pensive luster to a shallow brilliance, a murky light that, whether in a stone or an artifact, bespeaks a sheen of antiquity. . . . We do love things that bear the marks of grime, soot, and weather, and we love the colors and the sheen that call to mind the past that made them."

How rarely *we* applaud the sheen of antiquity, the patina of a life lived.

. . .

What about the undeniable sheen of youth, which the young so often fail to appreciate? How do we teach the young to accept, or embrace, imperfection?

My mother taught me so much about this. As is often the

case in families, my mother is the ballast in ours, the central force that has long enabled the rest of us to function, the strongest and wisest one. She is one of those remarkable people who possess both sense and kindness. She laughs at pomposity and self-importance, is more interested in thoughts than things, has little interest in money, and is simultaneously sharp-eyed and forgiving. She is also mischievous, which has resulted in some stunning pranks. When my older brother, then a politician, criticized our childhood lap dogs in an interview while declaring his preference for larger hounds, my mother, pretending to be the aggrieved president of the Maltese Appreciation Society, wrote him a letter complaining—to which he carefully crafted a response, not realizing it was her. She laughed about it for months afterward.

Mum has taught me so many crucial lessons. First, that grace—showing generosity and forgiveness even to those who do not deserve it—is not weak but extraordinarily powerful. Second, that kindness should not just be an aspiration but a daily practice, a muscle that, if exercised, can grow strong and become a habit or a way of life. Third, that sometimes you do not need to overthink resilience. For a psychologist, her philosophy is remarkably simple, yet effective: "You just get on with it." After one day, another comes, then another.

Mum also taught me that an enduring lack of vanity is a great gift to a daughter. This is not because grooming is inherently bad. It is because orbiting a woman whose self-esteem does not rest on applause for her appearance can show you that a million other things matter more. My mother has always been beautiful, with thick dark hair, blue eyes, and smooth skin. She has also always been fit, traveling a trajectory from Richard Simmons and Jane Fonda workout videos in the 1980s to Bikram yoga. (Possibly the best experiment was a Christian aerobics tape she bought called *The Firm Believer*.) But she is not in the slightest bit vain. And women who are not vain enjoy a freedom others don't. It is obvious that she measures herself, and others, in other ways. It is only now that I am realizing how rare this is, and how pleasant it is to be around.

A modest introvert with a big heart, Mum was never particularly preoccupied with herself, and has had a certain equanimity as a result. Just as Iris Murdoch wrote, happiness is being "busy and lively and unconcerned with self. . . . To be damned is for one's ordinary everyday mode of consciousness to be unremitting agonizing preoccupation with self."

Mum has been very unwell of late, and can no longer walk, but it has always been the case for as long as I can remember that whenever Mum enters a room, anxiety levels instantly drop; everything seems easier, calmer, cheerier. This was especially obvious when I had my first baby. I would be pacing with a bawling infant at midnight, racked with concern, and she would walk in, survey the scene, and we'd begin to laugh. So often I'd call her distressed about some drama, and halfway through my explanation of why I was upset she'd see the funny side and we'd start giggling.

She was, in short, phosphorescent, with a keen eye for the absurd. Once, my mother was working in Australia's most violent women's prison, Mulawa, as she did for many years, with a Christian group called Kairos. She was reading the Bible with some prisoners when one was told to recount the story of the women who saw Jesus after he rose from the dead. The inmate jumped to the task, ending with: "Well, then the woman turns around and says, 'Jesus, where the fuck have you been?'" Mum loved this story.

. . .

I do have my own vanities, of course. In my twenties, particularly, I was always struggling with the way I looked and cursing my shortcomings. I refused to diet but often exercised madly, running for hours upon hours, unable to extricate myself from a sticky kind of self-loathing. I now regret all the time I wasted worrying about my flaws, and realize that I should have been off hiking and exploring with my friends, refusing to sink into that kind of self-scrutiny that can screw with women's heads. I eventually learned to move with more ease in my skin after several long trips to India and Nepal, during which I danced for weeks on end at a Hindu-Sikh wedding, hiked through the Himalayas, stayed in old forts and palaces in Rajasthan with my free-spirited Indian friends, and was so fascinated by everything I saw that I forgot myself, and rediscovered joy. It can take a while, sometimes, to be the woman you want to be, and to excavate the misogyny or critical eye we too often internalize.

Vanity, for the most part, can lead to a great deal of unhappiness—and is unnerving to be around. People who are vain are usually more interested in what people around them think of them than who the people around them actually are. In contrast, Queen Victoria—and possibly Hatshepsut—for all their obvious faults, accepted their own physical limitations and were keenly curious about those around them. That kind of curiosity allows for absorption and connection, and is one of the best ways to undermine any anxieties about the way we look or where we might fall short.

When Barack Obama was asked if he was worried about his daughters dating, he told radio station WDCG in Raleigh, North Carolina, that he was "pretty relaxed." One reason for that, he said, was that his wife, Michelle, was "such a great example [in] how she carries herself, her self-esteem not depending on boys to validate how you look or, you know, not letting yourself be judged by anything other than your character and intelligence."

Just like my mum. It is supposed to be one of the greatest horrors a woman can contemplate, becoming like her mother. I can think of few things I would like more.

CHAPTER 9

Let Yourself Go

Once, while I was looking at an apricot-colored vintage dress at a stall on the Upper West Side of Manhattan, imagining myself in it drinking gin cocktails on the French Riviera, my then partner whispered in my ear: "You know, there comes a day when wearing old-lady dresses is no longer ironic."

Ouch. I was thirty-six. And apparently not even mutton dressed as lamb, but fast approaching jerky dressed as mutton, if we accept the dubious notion that the way women dress can be likened to the life stages of a sheep.

Deflated, I left that pretty dress hanging on the wire fence surrounding those markets on the corner of Columbus and West Seventy-sixth. But I still wear vintage.

So what does it actually mean to dress like an "old lady"? Or even just "dress your age"? Women are more often criticized for dressing like younger, not older, versions of themselves. When you reach forty, you're suddenly inundated with advice about "age-appropriate" wear. It doesn't happen to blokes in the same way, though they are stupidly often shamed for expressing any kind of creativity in dress, or for appearing to transgress any archaic gender rules, which is also limiting. Women have been wearing pants for far more than a century; when will we see men in any significant numbers wearing skirts? Women are expected to be vain; men are jeered at for showing even a passing interest in fashion, which is why terms describing fashionable blokes—"fop" (a man who is concerned with his clothes and appearance in an affected and excessive way), "coxcomb" (a man too proud of his appearance), and "dandy" (a man greatly concerned with smartness of dress)—so quickly become pejorative.

It is worth pointing out that one of the first recorded uses of "mutton dressed as lamb" was to praise, not ridicule, hot older women. In a lady's journal of 1811 the phrase was attributed to the future King George IV of England, who, when still a prince, was asked at a ball if he found a particular girl pretty. He snorted with derision: "Girl! Girls are not to my taste. I don't like lamb; but mutton dressed like lamb!"

The original intent of this phrase has been lost: Women are not praised for dressing like fabulous young things now. As we ascend the ladder of wisdom and maturity, we are cautioned to adopt restraint, to be "classic," "sophisticated," to eschew skin in favor of prim. And with every passing year, we are instructed to occupy less space and be more demure—and dull.

We are also told to monitor our appearance in a way men very rarely are. Find me a man leafing through a magazine that tells him to upturn his collar to hide his neck wrinkles, and I will upturn it for him.

One fashion guru advised women, "The worst thing you can do is to dress younger than you are." The worst thing! So bad, apparently, that a survey by online retailer isme.com suggested that 80 percent of Britons thought women should "start dressing down" when they turned fifty, and that a quarter of women over fifty were "scared of wearing high heels." Scared. Frightened.

After forty, we should, says a British fashion writer in *The Telegraph*, use plenty of conditioner on our hair and not risk a radical trim because "a bob at this stage could put a decade on you." Yikes! The author goes on to say a maxi skirt can also add "ten years." Get a haircut and the wrong dress, and bang—you're sixty.

One website also recently chided women over forty who wore tank tops, low-rise jeans, platform heels, bangles, and big earrings by asking, "Are you a middle-aged fashionista who just doesn't know when to quit?" Quit what, exactly? Are men in sharp suits ever called fashionistas?

Finally, we are told to smile more. "The sulky, not bothered expression which you may think cool (see Victoria Beckham) will in your 40s start to look sour," writes *The Telegraph*'s adviser. The answer? "Perk it up."

This mutton shaming has to stop.

Very occasionally, we are given permission to reveal

glimpses of our fleshly selves. A fashion journalist advised in *Harper's Bazaar* that mutton-ladies may still reveal morsels of skin—collarbones, wrists, and the back of the neck are safe "candidates for display. . . . All the places you'd wear perfume and would like to be kissed. It's about being adored, not ravaged."

All this nonsense is why I adore the funky octogenarians you can find on Instagram who proudly sport white hair, wild colors, sharp suits, massive sunglasses, and turbans. They refuse to fade, to hide, or to match their attire to the wallpaper.

My greatest mutton fantasy is just to wear and do what I want, and to not have such preoccupations even cross my mind. Isn't there a point when one can simply be a dowager, a grand old dame, a merry old boiler? When we can refuse to kowtow to prescriptions and permissions, and just march on in the shoes we fancy wearing?

Queen Victoria ditched suffocating corsets without blinking, much to the horror of her doctor. But who would elect to wear those things voluntarily? Instead, she wore exactly what she liked for half a century: mourning black, with diamonds.

I have long savored the prospect of letting myself go. It's just the most delicious concept: a balloon wafting into the ether, a raft flowing smoothly with the current. One day, I have imagined, I will find myself wandering along the street, either cheerfully unkempt with hair askew, or impossibly fabulous, wearing a curious assortment of clothes—perhaps a vintage frock with dapper heels—that meet just my liking. I might bump into an old acquaintance who will regard me with confusion. "Oh!" I'll exclaim, with an easy laugh, and, touching her arm lightly, I'll say, "I thought you might have known. I've let myself go!" Then I'll saunter off, dangerously liberated, feeling envious eyes on my back—having reached, finally, the age when you can reject rejection.

• • •

You have to wonder, too, if women are most free to let themselves go when they leave child-bearing behind them. I have only just discovered, while writing this, that the bones of women become aerated, filled with bubbles of air, and thinner, as they grow older, just like the hollow bones of birds.

Sometimes this makes them frail. But perhaps, also, this lightness of limbs enables flight. It allows us to let go.

• • •

I am not arguing fashion is in any sense trivial; only that unthinking parroting of it, and assumptions of conformity to it, are dull and limiting. Letting go should mean letting go of onerous conventions of dress, not of the joy of playing with fabrics and styles.

Not long before he died, the photographer Bill Cunningham took a photo of me at a New Year's Eve ball at the Metropolitan Opera in New York and placed it in one of his columns. As an unlikely candidate, I was honored: He was peerless, legendary, and so charming. But what struck me was the way he took the photo: He beamed, encouraged— "Yes, child," he'd say excitedly, repeatedly, "Yes!," quickly maneuvering from side to side as I stood smiling at him, infected by the eagerness that clearly had nothing to do with me and everything to do with him and his modus operandi. It was like getting swept up and spun around in a warm gust of air. He looked at his subjects—mostly women—with great approval and delight. No wonder *Vogue* editor Anna Wintour said, "We all get dressed for Bill."

Bill snapped thousands of women in his life, and he viewed them with an eye of appreciation, not judgment.

John Fairchild, former publisher of *Women's Wear Daily*, called him a "pixie on a bicycle": "You're at some dreary event. Suddenly, there's a flash, a wonderful word, and he just lifts you up." As Hilton Als wrote in *The New Yorker*, one of the things Bill Cunningham gave the world was "his delight in the possibility of you."

To Bill, fashion was not at the periphery but at the core of a purposeful life. "The wider world perceives fashion as frivolity that should be done away with," he said. "The point is that fashion is the armor to survive the reality of everyday life. I don't think you can do away with it. It would be like doing away with civilization."

So by "letting go," I don't mean relinquishing all attempts to be creative or colorful or fabulous with your clothes or your face, but quite the opposite: Do what you want with the way you look. After my surgeries, I am most of all just glad when my body actually works, and moves, and does not hurt. My daughter, though, has collected boxes of makeup and has strong opinions on fashion. Even my friends confess to being quietly thrilled if she compliments their clothes, so certain is her authoritative air. She has entered her teen years now, and I have so many things I want her to know, so many things I'd like her to remember if she stumbles into dark spots.

CHAPTER 10

Letter to a Young Woman

M y darling daughter,

I still have so much to tell you. I would never dare dictate how you must be, or what you must think, as you have such a firm sense of who you are—once, exasperated that people kept telling you "the apple doesn't fall far from the tree," you sighed heavily and said to me, "I want to *be* the tree." But after a life spent thinking about the often fraught yet glorious lot of women, I wanted to write these thoughts down for you.

First, demand respect, and give it. Sometimes, when you do this, you will feel insane, or be told that you are. Persist.

Use your brain. You will doubtless be praised for your sunny face, your kind ways, and your grace, but you must also always use, protect, and stretch your fine brain. Women threw themselves under horses, starved, marched, and fought for you to be able to speak and be honored.

Find friends with true hearts and love them long and loyally. Never take your family for granted; love them unwaveringly. Practice forgiveness on all of them.

Keep in mind that the most important quality in a person is goodness. If you ever decide to loop your heart to another's for life, make sure they possess a rare goodness, a decency that does not crumble under fire. Beyond the head-spinning intoxication and stomach-curdling craving, beyond the fireworks and first flames, goodness is what matters. Don't make the mistake of dismissing decency as dullness. A sense of safety might be rarer than you think. So, while we're talking about relationships . . .

Remember Stalin. Every young woman, on the cusp of the volcanic desires of adolescence, should be shown a photograph of the young Joseph Stalin. Before he became a dictator who murdered millions, he was a revolutionary and romantic poet with thick, foppish hair, intense dark eyes, and a handsome face—the kind of boy you might find yourself kissing in the back corner of a bar, oblivious to all eyes, clocks, and caution.

Google him. Young Stalin was hot. But clearly not a keeper, as he was also a brute, a tyrant, and a bad husband, who drank heavily, argued frequently, and flirted with other women. He addressed his second wife, Nadezhda Alliluyeva, with "Hey, you!" and arrested her friends after they told her he was butchering people. At age thirty-one, Nadezhda shot herself after a humiliating public fight with Stalin at a dinner party, during which he had flicked cigarettes at her. I wonder how different Nadezhda's life would have been if she'd learned how to X-ray charm, distinguish between passionate intensity and true love, and identify signs of aggression, manipulation, abuse, and control in even the most nascent relationship.

You know this is something I have reported on, a lot. At least we know so much more about which relationships to avoid than we did when I was a kid, when much violence against women was just "a domestic." But, still, you must avoid people who would control, criticize, or diminish you, in any way, or are jealous of you or make you feel small, or are drawn to your strength but then suck it dry. Stay with those who bring you comfort, understand you, and allow you to flower.

Know this, too: You deserve love. Real, enduring love. Buckets of it. Love is the greatest high on Earth. But remember Proverbs 4:23: "Above all else, guard your heart, for it is the wellspring of life."

Be You. Be the best version of yourself you can be. Work to understand—and show—what it means to have integrity.

Dare. Don't worry about what people think. Grasp every opportunity you are given and run at full pelt.

Don't let the world crush your astonishing spirit. Once, when you were about six, we had parked on the road opposite our apartment and you were in a bad mood, angry about something, or just hungry, I can't remember now. I was asking you to wait before we crossed the road, as I was scooping up your brother from the baby seat with one arm and gathering up groceries with the other. Repeatedly, I asked you to wait. Then I looked up and saw you walking across the road, slowly and deliberately. When you reached the middle, you turned, paused, placed a hand on your hip, and stared back at me. I called out sharply to you to watch the traffic, but inside I was torn: You were being such a little rotter, and putting yourself in danger, but the look on your face was pure pluck and rebellion.

Know that bad times will pass. They always do. Rubbish will get tipped into your life, occasionally vats of it, and sometimes this will be your fault and you must try to learn from it. But at other times it will be deeply unfair and all you can do is control the way you respond to it. Speak your piece but don't complain; draw yourself to your full height. Keep moving, place one foot in front of the other, and know it will pass. If it won't, do what you can to change it. But walk tall. Don't descend to nastiness and vitriol, ever. As Michelle Obama so beautifully put it, "When they go low, we go high." Find what makes you resilient.

Keep reading history. Actually, keep reading everything, but especially history—lives have been lived we can barely imagine. In that history you will find a seething mass of humanity that is always striving and reaching and falling and screwing up and being small and large all at once. You'll learn that basic rights can be rapidly eroded, and evil flourishes when good people look the other way. You will find that humans are capable of extraordinary tenderness and extreme brutality, all in the one day. That one person can contain breathtaking contradictions, sinners can have moments of greatness, and saints can have streaks of darkness. Understanding this is crucial, as you will come to recognize what it is you can accept in yourself and others. You will also see that character is partly innate and partly built: Make habits out of kindness, compassion, discipline, humility, and honesty. Work hard on them. This will give you an unseen and magical strength.

Buy a really beautiful dress—one that makes you feel like you could dance among the planets—at least once in your life, and wear it like a queen. Actually, buy more than one. When you were a toddler you were baffled by the idea that it wasn't normal to wear a tutu or sparkling frock every day of the week. Why stick your best clothes in the back of the closet, you thought, when you can saunter down the street in them this very day? We went out for "fancy" family dinners in the local café, and one night you ordered me to dress properly. Which is how I found myself walking up Columbus Avenue in Manhattan pushing your brother in a stroller, holding the lead of our dog, wearing a gold sequined minidress and trying to balance in my heels. You walked alongside with your father, beaming.

Listen hard. Show respect to every single person you meet, as well as those you don't meet. See the best in them. Be the kind of person who makes others feel better about themselves, the world, everything: Lift people up, don't tear them down. Try to understand what grace is, and how it can stitch together an abyss, and can conjure the unthinkable.

Never expect another person to support you. This will

free you. Find your purpose, or purposes, and live a life of meaning. Work hard to achieve financial independence, and buy a small place to live in as soon as you can.

Walk lightly on the earth. Be at peace with God. Never mock another person's beliefs. Allow yourself, and other people, to make mistakes. Accept your family for their frailties. Love your brother, as he will always be your greatest ally. Stare down bullies and don't walk past people in pain. But allow yourself to be vulnerable. Cultivate a sense of humor. Show mercy to yourself as well as others. Look at the world, and try to shift obstacles blocking other people's paths to equality and contentment, as well as your own.

When in doubt, uncertain of yourself and frustrated by everything, focus on other people. We have a saying in my family: "Some people are penthouse people and some people are basement people." In other words, encountering friends, or strangers, can be like hopping into an elevator. By the end of a conversation, or time together, you might feel lighter, happier, cheered. That's a person who takes you to the penthouse. Or you might feel strangely flattened, a bit down. That's a person who has taken you to the basement. Your Pa, your Nan, and your uncles are the former. You, too, should be a penthouse person: Uplift people and show them love; don't be quick to judge or criticize; look for the best in everyone; and remember what it is you share.

Lend a hand to anyone who needs it, and stand by those who are being trolled, or picked on.

Always buy the underpants that match the bras—without

guilt. Accumulate, slowly, beautiful or sturdy furniture, and surround yourself with things that you love. Delight in generosity; learn its joy. Pray, or meditate, often. Find the kind of art that thrills you, and drink it in. Dance as often, and for as long, as you like. Inhale music.

Be fair. I know I have told you this so many times, but truly: Treat other people the way you want them to treat you. Unless they are hurting you, being cruel to someone, or making people suffer, in which case you should run to safety or wither them to sticks with one of your stares.

Know you are loved. When you were born, the world rebooted and my heart permanently cracked open. It was like you had suddenly darted out of a portal from another world and landed on my chest, immediately staring into my eyes. You were instantly formed: Stubborn, funny, flamboyant, and confident, you defied anyone to stand in your way. I was wheeling you around Central Park when you said your first word—*dog!*—and I held your hand when you wobbled your way to your first steps.

You were never interested in crawling; you went straight up from the floor and into the world. I marveled, still do. I rode behind you in Paris when, even aged just eleven, your feet didn't touch the ground when you rode a bike along cobbled streets. It didn't deter you; you used walls as your brakes.

You have taught me so much. About certainty, confidence, style, and first-guessing. When you went through a lengthy phase of wearing your shoes on the wrong feet (mostly by accident), if anyone upbraided you, you'd stare back and say, "That's Poppy style."

You are so loved for exactly who you are.

Know that being a woman is magnificent. Soon you will be a young woman, blazing away on the Earth. Remember— as I learned from the "old ladies" at Garma—that your elders and ancestors give you an authority: the authority of being female in this world. Of being strong and certain and bold. Of being able to create and nurture life. There are a million ways to be a woman: Find your own and revel in it.

Shrug off anyone who would tell you to be less than you are. But perhaps I don't need to worry about that. A moment ago, I sent you a text message asking you if there was anything I needed to know about your day and you replied, "Yeah you need to know that I am awesome." And I wondered if—or hoped that—this might be the beginning of you demanding not praise, but respect.

PART III

Walking Each Other Home

The art of friendship: "I am here"

Author Ram Dass was born Jewish, but he considered himself an atheist until he began experimenting with hallucinogens with psychologist and writer Timothy Leary. Dass, known as Richard Alpert before an Indian guru gave him a new name, claimed that he "didn't have one whiff of God until I took psychedelics." He went on to explore a host of the globe's spiritual traditions, including Zen Buddhism, karma yoga, Sufism, Hinduism, and Judaism. But it is possible Dass will be remembered most for just one sentence he uttered: "We are all just walking each other home." It's a beautiful idea, and it's true.

It would be impossible to write a book about the things that sustain you when the world goes dark and not mention one of the greatest of these: friendship. Meeting wonderful people is luck; keeping them in your life takes thought, care, forgiveness, and devotion. Friendship is an art and a gift, and some people are brilliant at it. Best friendships can last from kindergarten to the nursing home, almost unchanged, and somehow keep you laughing. Being able to walk alongside the companions of your childhood, or youth, throughout your life, is a superlative experience.

My friend Jo, who loves music, food, and self-deprecation—and is one of the funniest people I know—met me for dinner at a Greek restaurant near my home recently. We drank red wine and talked about a book I had just given her, the novel *Burial Rites* by Hannah Kent, about the last woman to be condemned to death in Iceland in 1829, for an alleged murder. In the final pages, a priest called Toti rides alongside the condemned woman, Agnes, as she trudges to her death on her horse. Agnes is shaking and chattering uncontrollably with cold and fear, unable to move her legs when she climbs off. Toti says to her, repeatedly and simply: "I am here."

Jo began to cry as she spoke about the grace of the scene, and I realized that was what she had tried to tell me when she took weeks of caregiver's leave after my operations and sat next to me in different hospitals, watching me sink into pain then emerge again, looking haunted and half-dead, then staying at my house, cooking and trying to persuade me to eat, just to get me through another day: "I am here."

Sometimes it can be hard to be a companion, caregiver, or witness. But I will never forget those who were there for me and their concrete loyalty, and those who are there still.

And yet when I think about my friendship with Jo, I think mostly of joy. So much of it is defined by laughter, dancing, unending conversation, and escapes to a small fishing village on New South Wales's South Coast, where we explore the cliffs and deserted beaches of the untamed national park, climb over shipwrecks rusting on rocky shores, paddle along rivers and through mangrove swamps, and feast on freshly caught fish under wide skies as my kids explore rock pools.

We owe so much to our friends, each with their own story: those who have known us since we were children, those who joined the band along the way, those we met only fleetingly but who still stay with us, those who somehow manage to keep us alight. These people are the crossbeams of our resilience. Without them, I honestly do not know how I would live.

CHAPTER 11

Freudenfreude: Sharing the Joy

Jane Fonda told *Vanity Fair* that her female friends "keep starch in my spine." So do mine. Which is why I have never understood why some people hold on to a stubborn, unbending belief that women secretly loathe one another, and will scrap and brawl at the slightest provocation—catfight! I am not sure why this myth persists when female friendships are mostly incendiary, bulletproof, and enduring.

An Australian woman once wrote a book purporting to reveal "the truth about female competition," as though she were lifting the lid on a putrid worm farm. When I read these words I was stunned:

> Most women know, that as soon as their back is turned their female friends are checking out the size of their arse. If it's grown then it will be discussed among the other women in the group with glee. If it's shrunk then all sorts of hypotheses will be discussed. She's

bulimic, no, she's on cocaine, she's having an affair, no, she's definitely a lesbian, can you pass the cake? Gossip is powerful. Considered a form of female bonding, it involves . . . enjoying the short-lived glee of Schadenfreude and passing moral judgment on fellow females.

Women could still be feminists, she argued, while being competitive.

Now, I know women are entirely as capable of being jerks and bullies as men are. Women are, after all, human. But I was stunned because the obvious conclusion was omitted: Such women, or people, do exist, but you must not make them your friends; you must run from them (the best term for such creatures is "grimalkin"; it's now out of usage, but means "a spiteful old woman"). Seriously, run. Then, carefully, draw the brilliant, the decent, and the good-hearted near, and love *them* fiercely. Shed the toxic and the small; show loyalty and honor to those you love. It's not an accident; it's purposeful. Stand by your friends and spend time with those who'd rather swill acid than hurt you.

There are millions of excellent humans on the globe. Find them. Befriend them. Support them. And soon a plant with a thick trunk and roots will grow. Weed out those who spike conversations with put-downs, who are disloyal or unkind, who don't give you the benefit of the doubt and bad-mouth you to strangers. Because if you are mentally weighing your friends when they walk into a room, the question you must ask yourself is not "Am I a feminist?" but "Am I a dickhead?"

. . .

Gore Vidal, a man not known for humility or lack of ego, said that when a friend succeeds, "a little something in me dies." I disagree. People often talk about schadenfreude, delight in the misfortunes of others, but they seldom discuss its opposite, freudenfreude. One of the greatest, little-discussed joys in life is the way you feel when a friend takes off in flight.

I realized this when my friend Catherine Keenan was made Australian of the Year Local Hero in 2016. I sat at home watching the TV as, under a grim, gray sky that was spitting rain, then prime minister Malcolm Turnbull struggled to hold an umbrella over Catherine's head. Cath is the cofounder and executive director of the Story Factory in Sydney, which runs creative writing classes for underprivileged schoolkids, a quarter of whom are Indigenous. Housed in a building in Redfern known as the "Martian Embassy," the whole enterprise has seen the minds of thousands of young people, from seven to seventeen, bubble and erupt into poems, plays, essays, stories, and books, under the gentle eyes of more than a thousand trained volunteers.

On that night, eyes plastered to TVs and madly texting,

Cath's tribe was splitting with pride as we watched her walk across the stage to give her speech, still in shock, as the wind whipped her curly mane. As she then said:

> Telling stories is a fundamental part of being human. It's how we understand the world around us and how we convince others to work with us to change it. It is also—and anyone who sat with a child will tell you this—a profoundly and often wildly creative act. Telling stories is the way we take the complicated emotions and weird spirallings of imagination inside us and give them shape and form. It is how we show who we are to the world.

And it's hardly just an abstract indulgence, she added:

> We know the huge benefits of helping young people tell their stories. We know it because a growing body of research demonstrates the many and varied benefits that accrue for young people. They are more likely to go on to tertiary education, they watch less TV, they are more likely to volunteer in their community. I have seen it time and again. When kids are able to tell their stories, they stand just that little bit taller.

My chest hurt with pleasure watching her, and I began to think about why we so rarely acknowledge the joy of watching someone we love triumph—for example, when a friend is acknowledged for years of quiet, hard, important work, or finally lands a ball between goalposts and makes a dream concrete through determined effort. I was watching the same friend who had driven for two hours every week for six weeks to play with my toddler who was in the hospital with a broken leg, so that I could sneak off to the café downstairs and write my book on Queen Victoria; who cooked large piles of chicken schnitzel and cauliflower soup when I was ill myself, and has hosted numerous twelve-hour birthday lunches for all of us; who, when we were newspaper cadets in our twenties, was always the last to leave any party.

I could barely sleep the night of her award as I lay in bed thinking of the excitement in Cath's voice when she had called to tell me, as I was walking along a street in Philadelphia, that she was going to leave *The Sydney Morning Herald* and set up the Story Factory with lawyer, *Herald* colleague, and top bloke Tim Dick, after being inspired by U.S. author Dave Eggers's 826 Valencia, a creative writing center for under-resourced young people in San Francisco. I thought about the grueling months she had spent laboring on funding applications and wrestling with budgets, and the hours we had all spent painting the slats that formed the Martian Embassy walls, which were arranged in rows to create the illusion of being a portal to another world, the belly of a whale, or even part of a spaceship.

...

Buddhists call it *mudita*—a delight in another's good fortune, or an unselfish joy. The Yiddish word *nachas* has a similar meaning of pride in someone else's accomplishments, usually referring to one's children. Another slightly different but rarely used word with a similar meaning is "confelicity"—pleasure in another's happiness. In recent years, psychologists studying this concept have coined the term "freudenfreude" to describe the opposite of schadenfreude, and it means genuine rejoicing in another's success. I am not sure why we allow freudenfreude to be permanently overshadowed by its evil twin schadenfreude when it is equally useful as a word and a far superior emotion. Psychologists have found that freudenfreude is actually an effective bulwark against melancholia or sadness—a simple way, in other words, to get out of your own head and bask in borrowed sun.

Gore Vidal was wrong: It's not the success of our friends that is bad for us, but not relishing it. There is some evidence that a lack of freudenfreude can actually make you depressed. Experiencing it is something we need to work on; it's an attitude, or a habit of thinking, that we need to coax our minds into. We encourage people to feel compassion for those who struggle, so why not also encourage freudenfreude for those who triumph? It's the antidote to envy.

Psychology professor Catherine Chambliss has been studying freudenfreude for years. She conducted an experiment with severely mentally ill people in a residential psychiatric facility to try to establish if managing competitive impulses and friendship could help stem depression in a clinical setting. She and her colleagues spent time with staff and patients talking about how to consciously, deliberately, and genuinely celebrate the successes of other people, in what they called "Freudenfreude Enhancement Techniques." In her book *Empathy Rules: Depression, Schadenfreude, and Freudenfreude*, Chambliss writes that, while the strategy did not provide "a miracle cure," there were some startling results. For example, there was a "discernible positive influence on morale," the number of incidents of assault and self-injury declined, and the number of successful discharges "increased dramatically." Professor Chambliss concludes: "Empathy works wonders. Failures of empathy can be a big problem. Failing to respond with empathy to a friend's success or setback may prove toxic to relationships, undermining one's social support and possibly leading to social isolation and the depression it all too often produces."

In 2016, Professor Chambliss replicated her findings in a study in Europe, which found that students and hospital patients with depression had higher levels of schadenfreude and lower levels of freudenfreude. She and her co-author admitted that they did not know if these differences "might contribute to the development of depression, be a consequence of it, or both." At any rate, the connection makes sense.

The best part of any reality TV singing show is very often the family and friends backstage, screaming and hopping like rabbits when their candidate wins. It's the same at any sporting event, from the Olympics to local athletics carnivals, where the faces of parents and friends show uninhibited delight in a friend or loved one's success. Some researchers have dubbed this emotion "shoy," or sharing joy.

In one of Chambliss's studies, subjects who underwent Freudenfreude Enhancement Training were "more generous, less jealous, and less irritable" than those who did not. They were happier, too. In other words, a poor response to others' success or failure just ends up making you feel like rubbish. So, share the shoy. (A mutual obligation is at work here, too. The champions in our midst also need to not get too smug, and thank those who helped.)

...

I am not suggesting female friendships are always strawberries and cream; they can be intense, painful, and brutal, especially if they end abruptly. As Roxane Gay writes: "[You cannot] say women aren't bitches or toxic or competitive sometimes but . . . these are not defining characteristics of female friendship, especially as you get older." She adds: "If you find that you are feeling competitive, toxic or bitchy toward the women who are supposed to be your closest friends, look at why and figure out how to fix it and/or find someone who can help you fix it."

Yes! Because the rewards are enormous. Author Dan Buettner, who studied the "blue zones" of the world where people live longest, found that one common feature was strong friendships. In Okinawa, Japan, where, on average, women live to around ninety, people are placed into almost formalized friendship groups of about five when they are newborns. These groups are called *moai*, and the people within them care for one another for the duration of their lives, providing whatever kind of support is needed. Relationships may disintegrate and children riot and leave the nest, but friendships endure, and too often are unsung.

We rarely hear odes to the friends alongside us throughout our lives. This is partly why depictions of complicated, strong friendships—in TV shows like *Fleabag, Broad City, Younger, Parks and Recreation, Orange Is the New Black, Grace and Frankie, Unbelievable, Dead to Me, Sex and the City, The Handmaid's Tale,* and *Girls,* or in books like the elegant Neapolitan Novels of Elena Ferrante—gain such devoted, cultish followings.

English singer and songwriter Ellie Goulding wrote the song "Army" about her best friend, Hannah. She explained on Instagram:

I realized that I had focused a lot of writing on past relationships and it hit me I had never written about my best friend. The person I met in college over ten years ago. The person who was at my very first gig. The person who has seen me at my lowest and the first person I call in muffled sobs when something bad happens. We've been deliriously happy together, deliriously tired and deliriously sad together. I wanted to show our friendship for what it really is—honest, real, electric . . . the laughing at our own ridiculousness and foolishness, comparing our trials and errors, over-thinking our breakups and new loves, remembering everything we've been through to get to this point and being so proud of it. . . . We open our hearts up and take risks but together we are more powerful than ever. We are challenged every day but we see it through and sometimes it feels like we can conquer anything.

As she told Hannah, "When I'm with you, I'm standing with an army."

It's not about air punches or #squadgoals or Instagram boasts as perfected by Taylor Swift's old posse of spindly Amazonians. It's about a quiet knowledge that when one of your friends stands up on a cold, wet day in Canberra to speak about a dream she has fought for and made real, you stand taller, too.

My daughter has heard me bang on for years about my belief that choosing, and sticking by, loyal, decent friends is one of the most important things in life. What I'm waiting for her to understand is that by doing so, she isn't winnowing birthday party invitations. She's building an army.

CHAPTER 12

She Trashed Her Golden Locks

When I was a girl I had this strong feeling that I didn't
belong anywhere. . . . It was in my head, what I thought
and dreamed, what I believed. . . . That's where I be-
longed, that was my country.

— FROM *CLOUDSTREET* BY TIM WINTON

The most reliable way to judge my best friend Jock's state
of mind is by her hair. The first conversation we remember
having was about her colossal rope of a ponytail. It was thick,
blond, straight, and long, swung like a cartoon tail, and
brushed against my shoulders when we sat back to back at
our desks in sixth grade.

I had just returned from New York, where I had spent
most of primary school, and had unfortunately embraced
the feathered *Charlie's Angels* look then popular in my

neighborhood. This resulted in a limp, shaggy style that hung in my eyes; my pigtails were stumps.

One day, walking into my new school in Sydney, I saw that Jock—then known by her actual name of Jacqui—had not just chopped off her glorious hair, but had replaced it with a borderline mullet. I turned to her in astonishment: "Why did you cut off your hair?"

She stared back, almost scowling. "Fool," read her eyes. "What do I care for hair?"

I gazed back with quiet respect. We have been inseparable ever since.

When we were fifteen, floating around in a pool on the Gold Coast, I christened her Jock. It suited her. She was blunt, funny, and clever. She was always cooler and less sentimental than me. She walked away from hairstyles, relationships, everything, really, without blinking. On our last day of school I was red-eyed, hugging friends, fiercely promising we would always be in touch even though—sob—we probably wouldn't. Spent, I turned and saw Jock standing alone, staring toward the school gate. "Right," she said, sliding sunglasses onto her face, "Let's. Get. The fuck. Out of here."

I laughed. She was right; it was time. We'd never really felt like we fitted in. The suburbs we lived in were suffocating. It wasn't our families, which were close and—mostly—endured our late nights and four-hour phone conversations; it was the heavy atmosphere of convention and complacency along leafy streets that we burned to escape. Jock says what she remembers most is disapproval: a dense fog of disapproval we seemed to permanently inhabit.

Disapproval of our opinions: the boyfriends who told us, "You think too much." (Disapproval of our boyfriends, too, on whom opinions wildly varied; but who could turn from the furnace blasts of first love?)

Disapproval of our ambitions: the priests who told us women were meant to stay at home and submit to men; the church leader who showed his disapproval of the fact I had skipped youth group for a few weeks during my final school exams by saying, when hearing of my results, "It's good to come top of the state. But it's bad to burn in hell." The message was clear: Our brains, our lusts, our yearnings, our desires to stride the globe in large, firm steps—all were sinful.

Disapproval of the way we looked. When Jock shaved her head one day before a wedding, the only way to describe the looks on our friends' parents' faces was pure disgust. I stiffened and stared; she stiffened and looked down, reddening. The blushing rebel.

Disapproval of the ideas we explored, whether to do with feminism, racial inequality, or the shocking treatment of Indigenous people in our country. When I was seventeen, some elders took me out to a local coffee shop for ice cream and a hosing down: They were concerned about me, they said, concerned about my unpolished, poorly articulated but genuine desire to help improve the lives of the vulnerable. One woman placed her hands on top of mine, looked in my eyes, and said, "You know, ultimately social justice is a waste of time. Everything on this earth is." I so clearly remember my anger as I walked slowly to my car, a beaten-up white VW Beetle, slid in, placed my hands on the steering wheel, and accelerated away.

Disapproval of our clothes, especially mine: the retro suits and jackets, the long leather boots and fluffy coats. The friend who said primly, "You two look like you are always going to a nightclub." The relative who said, "You don't want to be like those girls who go clubbing all the time." But oh, we did. We wanted to dance. Every weekend, we would glide along railway lines as if they were banisters to the city, to find places where we could dance, eat nachos at five A.M., and wear ill-fitting vintage clothes that were a triumph of imagination over tailoring. We reveled in the freedom of the small hours when the clock stopped and our soles wore thin. Our parents said we were bad influences on each other; both families were regularly aghast at the crimes we committed against fashion. When I sent mine some photos from a backpacking trip to Europe, my older brother, then twenty-one and engaged, wrote to me: "All I am worried about is the guys and the clothes! But what's new?"

We danced like maniacs, many nights, for years, trying to shake off something we couldn't articulate, but often tried to, shouting over speakers, blinking through laser lights, carrying shoes along the sand of Queensland beaches at dawn. We never fought; we never tired of talking. We still speak almost every day, and I still get excited when I hear her voice: There's so much, always, to discuss.

We laughed that we were "dancing away the heartache" like Bryan Ferry. But now I think we were running toward joy. It was more like dancing away the odd feeling you get when you don't fit in where you live, where you don't agree with what you are taught, where argumentative girls and stroppy ladies are stuffed into asphyxiating boxes and told to mind their mouths. In church, we heard sermons warning of the lustful thoughts produced by holding hands, and instructing us that men were meant to be the heads of women at home and in church and that women were to learn quietly and submit to them—decapitated, for life, we ladies were.

We were trying to find another life, to find a kind of liberation of thought, to free ourselves. When we were on the dance floor, Jock's face was always dreamy, self-contained, and peaceful. Even after several hours of dancing, when some faces grow anxious, sweaty, fatigued, she was the cat with the dream of fresh cream.

But we were also told that to try to think your way out of psychological traps laid for women, to understand that one was not born but made a woman, was sin. I lost count of the number of times we were told that thinking such thoughts would make us unattractive to men, unmarriageable. As for homosexuality, that was unmentionable and viewed only as a sin, a certain shortcut to hell. Still is, where we grew up.

At the same time, we spoke for countless hours about feminism, and devoured Germaine Greer and Betty Friedan and Naomi Wolf along with D. H. Lawrence and Tennyson, Oscar Wilde, Patrick White, Kenneth Slessor, Judith Wright,

Les Murray, Alice Walker, Toni Morrison, Simone de Beauvoir, and Doris Lessing. We confided in each other about the crap we had to deal with just because we were women. The sounds and sights of unwelcome attention were a low-lying, persistent thrum throughout the years of our adolescence. The father of the kids I babysat who tried to grope me. The train station guard who cupped a fourteen-year-old Jock's breasts in his hands when she was walking by. The catcalling that switched in a second from "Hey, baby!" to "Fuck you, princess!" The law partner who requested sexual favors. The schoolkid who raped his sister, our friend. The uncle who abused his niece, another friend.

Around us, young women tried to shrink, to escape notice, to quietly gain control. Friends were hospitalized for anorexia and missed final exams. Jock and I both grew obsessed with food and complained repeatedly in letters, "I'm fat. I have become fatter." So often, the currency of conversation for women was self-deprecation and self-loathing; we all indulged in it: how stupid and ugly and unpleasant we were. It was a race to the bottom in an eschewing of confidence, a competition in self-hatred. So Jock and I took holidays where we read without moving as the sun circled the sky; we devoured everything we could about the lives and thoughts of other women, and understood what we were being taught was wrong.

The terms used by archconservatives for women talking about what it means to be a woman are boringly similar:

screeching, shrewish, shrill, strident. The word "strident" describes not just a point of view but a sound: a harsh, grating sound. Our opinions were strident because they were dissonant, discordant, unmusical. To the untrained ear, that was. To our ears, they were the beginnings of a song, and our friendship was the metronome, the steady clicks of company, assurance, and fire.

· · ·

When I went backpacking around Europe at eighteen, Jock and I wrote each other reams of letters full of ridiculous stories, lines from books we were reading and feverish laments about not fitting in. When we read through these recently, we howled with laughter. Jock wrote bluntly, in her drunken-fly scrawl, such gems as:

> I don't think there are very many people out there who think the same way I do, especially not 19-year-old Canadian boys.

> I've eaten chocolate for lunch and dinner yesterday and today.

> I love these empty nights, full of sound and fury and glitter and laughter and alcohol and gaiety and frivolity and money and these nights are slowly killing me.

Feeling pensive but wild. I need to do something very stupid tonight.

I'm going to buy myself a red cocktail dress. I don't give a fuck what it costs, it's just the idea. I don't care if I never wear it.

The Renaissance is an incredible era.

· · ·

In the quiet suburbs we lived in, women wore floral patterns; when attending church, some even carried wicker baskets with ribbons that matched their dresses. I am not making that up. The formal dresses were puffy and unflattering. It was little wonder we became fixated on Madonna, with her torn stockings, shoulder-baring T-shirts, obvious arrogance, and ripe sexuality.

I also became obsessed with history, especially World War II, and stories of women who, during the past couple of centuries, disguised themselves in men's clothing, becoming generals, soldiers, and priests, to escape the monotony and taboos of conventional female life. Jock and I had often worn men's suits, usually found in secondhand stores, for fun. We would turn up in tuxedos to dinner parties, and once went to a Marie Antoinette–themed twenty-first birthday party held in horse fields dressed in breeches, brocade coats, and white wigs. Women in uncomfortable corsets, hoop skirts, and high hair whirled around us. On the way home, my boyfriend turned to me, furious, and said, "Imagine if you saw two men walk in the door and one of them was your girlfriend." My eyes rolled in the dark.

In 1946, Anaïs Nin described men's clothes as a "costume of strength" in her book *Ladders to Fire*:

> "The first time a boy hurt me," said Lillian to Djuna, "it was in school. . . . I wept. And he laughed at me. Do you know what I did? I went home and dressed in my brother's suit. I tried to feel as the boy felt. Naturally as I put on the suit I felt I was putting on a costume of strength. It made me feel sure, as the boy was, confident, impudent. The mere fact of putting hands in my pockets made me feel arrogant. I thought then to be a boy meant one did not suffer. That it was being a girl that was responsible for all the suffering."

This was, of course, partly what Joan of Arc was burned at the stake for by the English—not just heresy against God, but also heresy against dress because she wore men's clothes. But Joan of Arc was not playing with fashion conventions. Before her imprisonment, she had practical reasons for cross-dressing—to conceal her identity, because a suit of armor did not easily fit over a bodice (and possibly even for "gender performative reasons"; in other words, she wanted to dress like a man so she could act like a man, at least in the ways in which men were then understood to appear).

After Joan's arrest, she continued to wear male cloth-ing—to protect herself against rape. According to the tran-script of her "condemnation," or show trial, presided over by carefully selected French clerics who were eager to under-mine any claim of Joan's to divine legitimacy, she wore two layers of clothing over her legs. The first layer was woolen hosen, fastened to her doublet with more than twenty thick cords. The outer layer was a pair of long, thick leather boots that jutted above her waist and were also looped tight to her tunic. Usually nuns watched over female prisoners, but male soldiers guarded Joan, a teenager whose virginity was made much of. Her frequent requests for a female compan-ion were denied, as was her request for protection from the church. She complained repeatedly that the English guards, as well as a "great English lord," had tried to rape her several times. (The court notary testified that this had been the case, and that she narrowly escaped one sexual assault be-cause an earl responded to her cries.)

Under questioning, Joan argued she had not breached any laws because medieval theology allowed for cross-dressing by necessity, when required for safety. One of the court's knights testified that he spoke with Joan many times when she was locked up in Beaurevoir Castle, and said that "many times too, in sport, he tried to touch her breasts, try-ing hard to put his hands on her bosom," though Joan pushed him away as hard as she could. In sport.

Imagine being burned alive because you didn't want to be raped. Or being cast as an evil witch because you *were* raped. Think of Medusa. We remember that she could turn men to stone with her rage, that she was monstrous and ugly and to be feared. But we forget, or are not told, that, as Ovid recounted, she had once been a beautiful maiden who was raped in the temple of Athena by the god of the sea, Poseidon. And for this, she was cursed and turned into a monster. Punished for being a victim.

. . .

When we were growing up, a typical way for men to dismiss—or try to cast as sinister—women's close friendships was to call them lesbians. This was often the case in aggressively masculine places, such as the pubs in coastal towns, especially in the great Temple of Slime and Sexual Harassment—Surfers Paradise in Queensland. Just our walking down the main street of that town—where the air was pungent with smoke and possibility and blokes clustered at entries to nightclubs or to eat burgers on the path—seemed to invite unending commentary on our sexuality, especially if we refused their enticing invitations to perform a variety of sex acts.

Jock wrote to me once about a book she was reading about attitudes, and slurs, that control female behavior:

The quote says, "When a woman hears this word tossed her way—lesbian—she knows she is stepping out of line. She recoils, she protests, she reshapes her actions to gain approval." But we never did, Jul. We arched our backs, sharpened our intellectual claws, linked arms gently and sauntered down Cavill Avenue, daring them, challenging them, provoking the cry "fucking lezzos."

This may have been how I missed the fact that Jock actually was a lesbian.

When we were about nineteen and studying at university, Jock grew her hair long again, and, alarmingly and uncharacteristically, started wearing modest dresses speckled with flowers. Just one floral frock was a screaming neon flag. She told me she was depressed; she complained about her weight. I failed to comprehend that she was pulling back into her past like a slingshot before launching forward.

Shortly afterward, she came out, and she lopped her hair off in giant chunks and dyed it platinum. Not long after we turned twenty (our birthdays are two weeks apart) I wrote to a friend in New York: "Jacqui has just had her hair cut. . . . So many guys said to her they wouldn't talk to her if she had short hair, 'Keep it long, it's so pretty,' and half out of spite, she trashed her golden locks."

Jock zipped herself into short shiny dresses and slid into the queer community with a joyful exuberance: She had found her tribe. I tagged along with her as she dived into another world, which was a true revelation, one of joy, acceptance, and a blurring of identity that we, even as white middle-class girls from the suburbs, had craved—especially, of course, Jock. In the heaving, grinning masses of people dancing on pavilion floors, wearing beautiful, eye-bogglingly creative costumes, in all the sweat and delirium and joy, it did not matter who we were or where we came from or what we thought. It was delight.

Jock's hair turned black, red, brown, white blond, wispy, cropped, pixie. I toyed with streaks. Then she fell in love, intensely in love, with a leather-clad girl called Josie who had curly black hair, thick chains around her neck, and eyeballs that burned attitude across crowded rooms.

Until then I had been the one to tumble sideways into consuming relationships and emerge, hair electrified, after a couple of years; Jock stifled yawns and shrugged off boyfriends like loosened capes. Now she cartwheeled happily into her new love, reappearing for only brief moments to telegraph her joy.

Her hair didn't change much, ever again. She had found another life.

Meanwhile, I turned from my law studies to write a PhD, and kept writing, working, and studying until I was able to return to the country where I had my first and worst haircut, the country I had always known I would return to: America. First I went to Boston alone, as a fellow at Harvard, then I went to work at *Newsweek* with the brilliant writer and editor Jon Meacham, dragging along my baby daughter and then husband to New York. I slid into a job I loved, working alongside nerdish editors and journalists who shared my obsession with history, religion, and politics. Opinions, the currency of our work, were welcomed, devoured, and dissected, the more irreverent and counterintuitive the better. It was intoxicating. I was overwhelmed by an unfamiliar, instant sense of belonging. I was happy.

A few months after arriving, I found myself walking down Lexington to a hair salon on East Fifty-sixth Street and unwittingly blowing my weekly budget on a cut.

I looked at the hairdresser: "Cut it all off. Make it edgy? Whatever you like."

For the first time in my life, I had short hair.

• • •

Sometimes it is hard to know if home is where you return to or where you start from. It is intangible things: people, not postcodes, and conversations, not couches. When you start from a place, with a friend, you will find you are bound not to the suburbs you grew up in but to the person or people you left with. And these skeins of friendship, knitted by billions of words over decades, bind, then act like kites, allowing us to soar while knowing we can return to talk to someone who will remind us we were not just fools with shaggy hair who danced marathons to escape monotony and restraint, but also women who were escaping strangulation; who will tell us that it's okay to run, stumble, fall in love, cry, make mistakes, dye your hair red, want to write, or want to be a full, equal, complicated human being, that it's okay to dream of more. To want to "Get. The fuck. Out of here."

And they will understand that what you might have been looking for was not another suburb, or even just an exit sign, but open skies, the skies dreamed of by thinking women for centuries. And that the impulse to run is the same as the impulse to run a clipping razor across your scalp: It's an impulse for freedom. We shed hair in a bid to shed skin.

In this way, feminism can, for millions of women, be a primer for phosphorescence; it peels off layers of rotten thought, of negativity, or narrowness, confinement, and entrapment, and allows us to be our true, complicated selves, to be independent, to relish liberation of thought and revel in reinvention, while reminding us of the magnificent, long lineage of women, our predecessors and ancestors, who have insisted the world can be better. It prevents the too easy snuffing of our lights with assaults on our brains, bodies, self-esteem. It allows us to erect the architecture of our thinking about who we are.

Throughout it all, Jock and I have remained steadfast, shoulder to shoulder. A couple of years ago, when I was asked to speak at the end-of-year speech night at our old high school, I emailed Jock to ask if she wanted to come. She responded: "Mate, any chance to sing [our old school anthem] 'Kindle the Flame' again and I am THERE. Reserve my seat. Book hair and makeup. Oh also I am blond again."

When, in recent years, I have been ill, it is Jock who has been by my side, squeezing my hand as I get wheeled into operating theaters, laughing at my incoherent rambles when

I come out of the druggy hazes and hallucinations afterward, guarding my bedside to make sure it is free of drama and crowds, bringing me shampoo and food supplies, making sure there is someone to walk my dog. She has repeatedly taken caregiver's leave to spend time with me in the hospital, flown to different cities when my treatment has taken me there, sat by my side during consultations with surgeons, head bent, brow furrowed, taking notes. Sometimes, I know, it has been hard for her to stomach the grief and anxiety, but she persisted, trying to hide her concern and darts of sadness. Her pragmatism and humor have kept me sane. When we were teenagers, our families used to say we were bad influences on each other; I quietly crowed when my brother recently called her an angel.

She is just a glorious creature—and has been with Josie for twenty-five years. I am so proud; a relationship like theirs is rare, and golden. They married in Washington—before it was legal to marry in Australia—Jock beautiful in a red dress, leopard-print shoes, and neatly combed blond hair. We have dinner every Tuesday and speak most days. The second I heard Australians had voted a thunderous yes to the question of whether same-sex couples could marry, I called her and we both cried.

CHAPTER 13

Burning Bright: Candy Royalle

Why is it that some people can live alongside us for decades, in schools, office cubicles, houses, apartments, but barely leave a trace, while others, whom we know only briefly, alter us indelibly? You know the kind: They pass like cyclones flashing light—thunderous, brief, unstopping—while scorching marks on our lives.

This was my experience with Australian writer and performer Candy Royalle, who died in 2018. She was only thirty-seven. We'd met only a few weeks earlier, but we immediately sparked and spoke for hours about poems, unheard voices, the beauty of community, the way words can spool from trauma, cancer, and an insistence on love. We spun dreams around a national poetry competition for women, one that I wanted her to judge. I instantly loved her spirit; it was luminous, generous, fierce, and sharp. When I heard she had died, it felt like a meteor had ripped through my gut.

Only two weeks before, Candy had performed onstage

with her band the Freed Radicals at the Red Rattler in the Sydney suburb of Marrickville. That night, I was unsure whether to go. It was cold and rainy, it was an hour's drive across town, I needed to find a babysitter, and all of my friends were busy or lazy. Then I reread her email: "It would mean a lot to me if you came." So I did. And to my surprise, within five minutes of my creeping in to perch on a stool in the middle of the theater, tears were rolling off my chin. She spoke of love, and lust, and hurt, and injustice and suffering and art, as well as the betrayal of her body. It was like watching a flame; she blazed.

Candy had been having treatment for her third bout of ovarian cancer and had to sit for half of the performance— when she was not dancing—and she told us of the rage, anguish, and vulnerability of being ill. I had been cut open like her, too, and we had spoken about the scars that spanned our torsos. "How could you love me," she cried that night onstage, "with a scar like this?," then bit her lip and turned to dance. I realized with a jolt that I had wondered exactly the same thing.

In one poem, "Birthing the Sky, Birthing the Sea," Candy spoke of yearning to live:

> She doesn't want to live forever
> Just long enough to be able to love a little harder
> To become a little smarter
> To heal the world just enough that
> evolving hearts have a platform from which to start.

The room roared with love; she was buoyed by it for days.

Though I barely knew her, I had found a poet whose words were like jumper cables on my life. Candy taught me that even the briefest of encounters matter and that we should cherish them; that the voices from the margins are crucial; and that poetry matters, intensely.

When we talk about poetry, we too often think of men who lived long ago in far-off lands, or about the wars of generations past. We don't think of a thirty-seven-year-old woman dancing to a tune of her suffering and daring us — in the very last breath of what we did not know would be her final performance — to call it art. Candy, born Cindy Malouf, wrote about being a "bold, queer Arabic woman" who struggled with a sense of not belonging — until she found the big, devoted, disparate, creative tribe that is mourning her now. This tribe, she said, lives in the "Borderlands." As Candy wrote, "We utilize things like art and activism to create a place of belonging within the margins and can revel in what it means to be an outsider who belongs."

Their work rarely airs in the mainstream media, but so many poets today, especially those from diverse communities, whether Indigenous, migrant, Muslim, queer, or other, are marked by contagious passion, obvious in the spoken word events that have sprouted like toadstools in recent years. Their storytelling unravels truths.

In May, Candy wrote to me about the ways she had witnessed poetry change lives, "as a tangible, actual thing." At one school workshop, she said, held over several days, a young Islander girl's family was going through a really hard time. . . . It got so bad, she ended up in a shelter for a few nights, but she made sure she was at that workshop every day. . . . A few months later she wrote to me to tell me that meeting me, getting to write, engaging with poetry, had literally saved her life. That she had been at risk of self-harming and if we hadn't been working with her during that time, she doesn't know what she would have done.

During her last five years working with young Aboriginal people in Nowra, in New South Wales, she said,

many have expressed that poetry has been the thing that saved them. I have witnessed them live through the suicides of many people they love (often teenagers as well), police harassment, physical abuse and other traumatic experiences, but day in and day out they attend the workshops and mentoring sessions because it helps them give voice to their lived experiences.

I think this is the most powerful thing about poetry. Everyone has a voice, and yet not all those voices have an avenue or a platform. Poetry is a tool to give those voices power, a place to channel trauma (and joy), a platform [from which] to be heard in a world that is often deaf to marginalized voices—those voices we actually need to hear most from.

She said it was "no accident" that 90 percent of those who came to her adult classes were women who'd experienced great trauma. "The very act of writing and sharing is one of catharsis. It's important to remember the sharing part, too—poetry made for the page tends to stay there. Work written to be shared helps us rehumanize the dehumanized—whether it's our own stories we share, or the stories of others."

What a beautiful woman.

"She doesn't want to live forever," Candy chanted when she last stood onstage, frailer than we knew, in a tiny red theater being hammered by rain. "She just wants the world to know she was a hurricane and not a zephyr."

. . .

My friendship with Candy stamped my life. It was a fragment of time, but it was enough to jolt my spirit; it was a naphtha-flash of lightning, an insight, a connection, as misused and banal as that word now is. We had both been torn in two, resected, and stitched together again—we were "almost mythical now," as she said. We both loved words, and wanted to amplify the quiet, unheard voices. It was a pure kind of bond, one that people who feel like, or are, outsiders, tend to appreciate and treasure most acutely. To find each other, we just have to be open to finding others, and also, I think, to art and creativity and poetry, to be able to build, and cross, those slender bridges of community, and of hope.

When Australian musician Nick Cave's teenage son fell to his death off a cliff in Brighton, England, Cave said it was his community of fans that enabled him to continue. He wrote: "I felt very acutely that a sense of suffering was the connective tissue that held us all together. Without being hyperbolic, this feeling of collective love has saved my life. It is a transcendent circle that just seems to grow stronger. It is religious." The key to living, he says, is to try to "actively reduce each other's suffering." This is also "the remedy to our own suffering; our own feelings of separateness and disconnectedness. And it is the essential antidote for loneliness." I strongly agree with this. If your heart is sore, and you cannot soothe it, turn to help or open up to another, and in doing so you may happily forget yourself for a while.

· · ·

Sometimes, even complete strangers can give us unexpected comfort. One day recently, I went into hospital for a scan I had been dreading. It was three months after my third surgery, and I was still in severe, untouchable pain on most days. It seemed I had developed a complication, and it was hard not to be anxious that the cancer had somehow rapidly returned. (It hadn't.) I decided to go on my own, and relieve my friends from yet another hospital visit.

I was standing at the front counter waiting to check in. The woman next to me was trembling and apologizing to the receptionist: "I'm so sorry; I am feeling nervous." I reached across, put my arm around her, and squeezed her shoulder.

I was then ushered into a windowless room with a row of armchairs, where a nurse draped a blanket over my legs as I sat down. Another nurse came to put a cannula into my arm but made a mess of it: She lost the vein but kept jamming the needle in, forcefully, until blood spurted out. To my embarrassment, tears began running down my cheeks from the shock of the pain as she apologized and tried again. But I cry so rarely that once I had begun, I could not stop.

I walked around the corner, sat on one of the chairs outside the scanning room, and cried. All the pent-up fear—often called "scanxiety" by cancer sufferers—flowed out. Then the woman I'd met at reception, a middle-aged mother with a kind, weathered face, sat down next to me with urgency, grabbed my hand, and said, "Look, love, this happens to me all the time. Boy, you should see me when I lose it—I really lose it, I go off. Let yourself cry. Go on, have a good blubber."

My new friend, Deanne from Dubbo, kept a firm hold of my hand and talked in a stream as I stared at her, red-eyed. She knew what it was like, she said. She had been a single mother with cancer—breast and then lung—and was still going. She was very proud of herself for giving up alcohol, but quitting cigarettes, which she had become addicted to as a twelve-year-old trying to quell hunger pains when out gathering sheep, was harder. She told me I looked thin, and gently scolded me for trying to tough it out on my own. She told me to learn to rely on my friends more. "You look like you're always the strong one," she said, "but you have to know it's okay if sometimes you are not." I nodded.

We walked out after our scans were over and during the removal of our cannulas it dawned on Deanne—who had traveled fourteen hours to get to the hospital—that she could now break her fast. Her eyes glazed as she contemplated her options out loud, before deciding upon barbecue chicken. She grinned at me and waved goodbye. As she walked through the large swinging doors to the exit, I could still feel her fingers gripping mine.

PART IV

———•—•——

Invincible Summer

Regarde: *Look, and savor*

In the midst of winter, I found there was, within me, an invincible summer.

—ALBERT CAMUS, "RETOUR TO TIPASA"

For years I had one word stuck above my writing desk, a quote from the French writer Colette: *"Regarde!"* "Look!" Look around you. Forget your own ruminations, and drink in what you see. Colette's mother, Sido, had instructed her to carefully observe the world and savor it. *"Regarde,* little darling, the hairy caterpillar," she would say, "it's like a golden bear! Oh! *Regarde!* The bud of the purple iris is opening! Come quick, or it will open before you can see it." *Regarde* became Colette's credo: Look, wonder, feel, live. As a child, she would wake at 3:30 A.M. and wander in the woods near her house in northwest Burgundy, drinking from hidden springs and gathering strawberries and gooseberries in large baskets. This intense curiosity about the natural world endured to the end of her life.

This was especially the case with flowers. In her last days, in Paris in 1954, Colette recorded a message for students that began: "Throughout my existence, I have studied flowering more than any other manifestation of life. It is there for me that the essential drama resides, and not in death, which is just a banal defeat." Friends took her out to see the buds of spring, and she leafed through illustrated books of insects and flowers, asking to have her butterfly specimens taken off the wall so she could look at them more closely. On the afternoon before she died, she was looking through a book of lithographs with a friend as swallows swarmed outside her window in anticipation of a thunderstorm. Judith Thurman writes in her masterful biography, "The sky was as heavy as a pot cover. . . . With a sweep of her arm that embraced the rustle of live wings in the garden and the images on the page, Colette spoke her last coherent word: '*Regarde!*'"

By keeping the word *Regarde* scrawled on a fading yellow note on my wall in my twenties, I was trying to remind myself to—as Australians would put it most bluntly—get over myself, and look around. Regarding, more than anything, is a huge relief: Imagine all we would miss if we kept tripping down the infinitely curling internal and interminable staircase of self-examination. The word was also a constant reminder to wonder and to savor—something my son has also taught me, and something that I now see as a key to quiet joy.

Illness or isolation can clear the air for this kind of contemplation. When you are ill, you gaze at the healthy, wondering why they don't bound about with unrestricted joy every hour, why they take the simplest of pleasures and functions for granted: feeling hungry, eating a meal, keeping food down without vomiting, having functioning organs, planning retirement, dreaming of a future.

What you do is think, and watch. You sit or lie in your bed, on a couch, or on a hospital trestle and think. As the formidable English social theorist Harriet Martineau wrote in 1844 in her book *Life in the Sick-Room*, "Nothing is more impossible to represent in words . . . than what it is to lie on the verge of life and watch, with nothing to do but to think, and learn from what we behold."

We need to learn how to regard and pay attention, to mine our inner strength, and accept the possibility that we can emerge from pain and grow by moonlight in times of darkness—that we can push "right back" on winter and find inside a summer. The way to faith, hope, and purpose are not to disregard the world, or the facts of our lives, but to observe them more acutely. We also need to seek and settle upon a purpose in life—something many people seem to discover once they fully open their eyes.

It's in this way, I believe, that we can become phosphorescent.

CHAPTER 14

Thoughts for My Son: The Art of Savoring

I have discovered that it is enough when a single note
is beautifully played.
—ARVO PÄRT, ESTONIAN COMPOSER

There are so many things I want to teach my son. To stand like a tree; to be true; to respect women as equal and also as magnificent, flawed, real human beings; to be kind; to understand the depths and shallows of the seas; to forgive fools; to carefully collect the good-hearted like shells on a beach; to find the part of the natural world that most brings him joy and explore every corner of it.

To file his taxes on time and learn to breathe properly over and under water, to be humble, to fold things the right way because I still get it wrong, to scrub barnacles from friendship when they form, to love his family fiercely and never take them for granted.

To find a purpose and honor it, to look for commonality with every person, to laugh at himself often, to hunt awe, to value silence and the discipline of logging off, to find ways to love his enemies, to learn to cook some things that make people happy, to eschew perfection, to seek the divine.

To dance whenever possible, to keep walking in rain and sleet and snow, to learn self-reliance, to not waste a second on the jeers of cynics or the jibes of hateful people, to endure, to run and meander and swim and travel and allow himself to make mistakes and be honest with everyone and himself. And to recognize that even in the madness, the toxicity, the decay and rot of the world, music is made, and played, and danced to.

That, as Aslan revealed in C. S. Lewis's *The Lion, the Witch and the Wardrobe*, behind every earthly law is a deeper magic that defies logic: a forgiveness of the unforgivable, a selfless gesture, a moment of grace. That this grace fuels galaxies, that the sun powers the planet and the moon pulls the tides, but the universe is largely unknown, spinning and vast, and that in itself is an ode to curiosity.

That he should study the craft of mathematicians, but also listen to the poets and learn from the bards. That he should respect the sixty-thousand-year history of his country, listen to the lament of its original inhabitants, recognize their rightful, central place in our land, and lean against those who would block, mute, resist, or diminish them.

And that's just a start.

But the older he gets, the more I realize how much he is

teaching me. He has what American poet Jack Gilbert would call a stubborn gladness. He's only eleven, but he delights in life, and it's contagious. When he was a baby, peekaboo was the finest joke on the planet. Now the greatest moments of his life have been: 1. When he had a bowl of delicious pasta, plain, with olive oil, on the Gold Coast. 2. When he had a ball of raw pizza dough in Washington, D.C. This was, for him, the highlight of a trip to America. He often fondly recalls that ball.

The rule at our dinner table is that every child must ask every visiting adult two questions, so that they learn to think about people around them instead of just batting away cli-chéd questions like "How is school?" Often they ask about the day friends had, or what color they like most, or the meal they'd eat if only allowed one more for the rest of their lives. But frequently my boy gets weird. As his godfather, Woody, told me, "He thinks sideways." One recent question was: "If you were a piece of ham in the fridge and you had to find your way out of the house and get past the cat to go to another country, how would you do it? And you can't walk and you don't have arms; you can only wriggle." Then last night: "If you were a hamburger fighting a burrito, what strategy would you use to defeat it?"

When he was a toddler he developed the habit of going around the dinner table and asking everyone what their favorite part of the day was: "What yo' fav' part day?" Around we'd go, then he'd launch again: "What yo- second fav- part day?" Inevitably, his answer would be that exact moment.

We could go to Disneyland, glide along several miles of water slides, jump on enormous trampolines, or eat ice cream at the beach, but his answer would almost always be "Dinner here now with all of you."

What I really want my son to know is that life, with all its striving and seriousness, its cerebral quests and spiritual yearning, is contained in crisp red apples and white-marble moons, furry caterpillars and leopard-spotted slugs, the slobbering of excitable dogs, laughter, the crashing of waves, the sighting of a seal beneath a cliff or of a cuttlefish on a reef, the scent of jasmine after a morning swim, a steaming bowl of fresh pasta, the smell of a just-baked cake — that all these jostling, bobbing moments sustain us, that they are the string that threads our days.

But if I am completely honest, this is what he is already teaching me.

. . .

Social scientists refer to this enjoyment of happy moments as savoring. The crux of savoring is paying attention to pleasure. Fred Bryant, who wrote a book on the subject, describes it as "like swishing the experience around . . . in your mind." Bryant, associate professor of organizational behavior at Esade Business School in Barcelona, has crystallized the research on how to savor around three recommendations: Look forward to something; enjoy it when it occurs;

and reminisce about it afterward. I know, it sounds bleedingly obvious, but the point is that if you aren't born a natural savorer, you can still cultivate the practice.

The actions are simple. Eat slowly. Don't get distracted. Be present. Look for something beautiful on your daily walk. Don't waste time faultfinding, or dwelling on mishap. Avoid negative people. (This is hugely important, and not a simple task. You have to actively work to root out people from your life who see only shade in light. Be careful before drawing them close.) Tell friends when you hear good news. (Alarmingly, some savoring researchers suggest allowing yourself to jump up and down when excited, but treat this counsel with caution: Tom Cruise comes to mind.) Throw a party to mark your achievements—or someone else's. Explore meditation. Embrace irregularity.

The only time I was ever thrown out of a lecture at university was when I was having a tug-of-war with a jelly snake in first-year economics with my friend Jeremy, a man with an unmatched love for life's micro-pleasures. All Jeremy needed to be happy was food, beer, and a decent swell. When we were housemates in Bondi, the first thing he would tell me about every day was his lunch. He'd walk in the front door and get straight to it: "Oh, Jule, I had the most incredible kebab. Unbelievable. I don't know how they make it taste so good!" He'd then describe the layers, textures, sauce, and toppings, and I'd laugh. It was infectious. What I didn't know then was that this tendency to keep talking about a meal for hours afterward indicated a strong ability to savor, to hold on to a positive emotion long after it first takes hold.

Jeremy still does this, by the way. He has a young family now, and when I called recently they were out at dinner. "Jez! How are you?" I said.

"Oh, Jule, so good. I'm having a pizza. It has the most perfect crust, it's amazing: half Neapolitan, half something else; it's an Italian family and they make their own sauce, with this melted cheese—seriously, you have to try it." I guarantee he bounded into work and told his colleagues about it the next day. Others would eat it and forget it straightaway.

My mate Woody is similar. He has devoted his life to hunting awe—it is the DNA of our friendship. He has spent years researching in oceans, deserts, and parks; and writing books about wombats, great white sharks, ancient pine trees, the Great Barrier Reef, and dog fences. He dives, catches waves, rides bikes, runs for hours with his beautiful border collie, Ringo, and builds his own houses on huge, quiet stretches of land nestled between the sea and rain forest. Very often when I call him, he is perched on a tractor doing something on his property, short of breath. I regularly get text messages about the sighting of an owl, or the perfection of a bath he has placed in the middle of his woods, and he sends me photos of hatching turtles and sunsets, which I repay with shots of cuttlefish, my daft dog, and various underwater adventures. And yet he is also a master of savoring the small things. The single part of every day that makes him happiest is the English breakfast tea that he brews first thing in the morning with freshly grated ginger. He doesn't need social scientists to tell him that this is a healthy sign of an ability to savor; the early morning grin on his face gives it away.

...

A string of studies have examined the characteristics that make us more or less likely to be able to savor, with one such study even going so far as to posit the theory that determining what separates a person who savors good things from one who doesn't may unlock some of the biological mysteries associated with depression.

One of the keys to happiness, it seems, is having a low bar. My younger brother, Steve, an unflappable, gentle, much-loved man, had the following motto for his wedding: "Expect imperfection." If things go wrong, he said, so be it. And of course the wedding was glorious, and if things went wrong I can't remember them.

In a study conducted by the University of London in 2014, participants were given small amounts of money to gamble. Those who did not expect to win were the most excited when they did. "The secret to happiness," said psychologist Barry Schwartz, "is low expectations." Or at least realistic ones, erring on the low side.

The Danes have long known this. In 2006, epidemiologists from the University of Southern Denmark tried to ascertain the reasons the Danes regularly come top of the list of the most satisfied people in Western countries. Professor Kaare Christensen and his team concluded: "If expectations are unrealistically high they could be the basis of disappointment and low life satisfaction. While the Danes are very satisfied, their expectations are rather low." Take this Danish newspaper headline, for example, reporting the latest survey marking their good cheer in 2005: "We're the happiest *lige nu* [just now]." Professor Christensen described this as the sentiment "for the time being, but probably not for long and don't have any expectations it will last." Don't assume this moment will happen again; relish it.

Conversely, driven perfectionists may struggle to savor simple pleasures. A 2014 study of how much undergraduates had enjoyed their last vacation found that Type A personalities were less likely to savor than Type B personalities, partly due to perfectionism. The authors reported: "Findings revealed Type A's focus on how proud they are and [how] impressed others are, but are only moderately to weakly involved in actively storing positive memories for later recall, or in reminiscing about prior positive events." This may be, the authors suggested, because they are impatient to move on to new opportunities, or reluctant to spend time "encoding memories at the expense of striving toward future accomplishments."

Another influencing factor may be a person's practice of

discipline. Not surprisingly, the concept of savoring has been frequently tested with one of the greatest of pleasures: chocolate. In one study, the group was divided into those who could eat chocolate any time they wanted, and those who had to abstain for a week. The fact the abstainers were so thrilled to be eating chocolate again was heralded as testimony of the merits of occasional self-denial. Asceticism, the authors concluded, has benefits for happiness, even in rituals like the Christian observance of Lent, fasting for Ramadan, or New Year's resolutions. Even just increasing a person's subjective sense of how long it has been since they have eaten their favorite food can make them happier to eat it.

People who think they are particularly deserving of happiness—and we all know a few of these—are less likely to be able to savor. A 2016 Case Western Reserve University study found that entitlement—"a personality trait driven by exaggerated feelings of deservingness and superiority"— can lead to an unending cycle of negativity. Lead author Joshua Grubbs said: "At extreme levels, entitlement is a toxic narcissistic trait, repeatedly exposing people to the risk of feeling frustrated, unhappy and disappointed with life." Narcissists will promote themselves as hugely optimistic, ready to conquer and control, yet when they cannot, they crash. It's a fragile optimism.

It seems wealth can also be a roadblock to savoring, as a sense of pleasure can be dulled over time by repetition and

abundance—even when it comes to enjoying small pleasures like chocolate, which in one study rich people ate
more quickly and enjoyed less.

Psychologist Daniel Gilbert coined the term "experience
stretching," meaning in one sense, as Jordi Quoidbach puts
it, that "experiencing the best things in life—such as surfing
Oahu's famous North Shore or dining at Manhattan's four-
star restaurant Daniel—may actually mitigate the delight
one experiences in response to the more mundane joys of
life, such as sunny days, cold beers, and chocolate bars."
You don't even have to actually go to these places to bring
this about—just *knowing* you can go can dull the savoring:
"In other words, one need not actually visit the pyramids of
Egypt or spend a week at the legendary Banff spas in Canada for one's savoring ability to be impaired—simply knowing that these peak experiences are readily available may
increase one's tendency to take the small pleasures of daily
life for granted."

And there are so many things to savor, right on our own
doorsteps. The artless laughter of a toddler; the smell of the
grass after rain (petrichor); the perfect poise of a raindrop on
a stem; an explosion of cherry blossoms; lakes reflecting sky;
red dirt; your sleeping child's cheek mashed against a pillow
as they sleep; fresh sheets; music; heavy rain on the roof; a
little hand reaching for yours; falling autumn leaves; an
endless summer night; an orchestra tuning; faces of proud
parents in stands; lights dimming before a play; the cup of
tea made at just the right strength, with the perfect amount

of milk, at the correct temperature; squeezing through crowds to the perfect concert spot before a stage; singing in a choir; the warbling of a magpie; the curved limbs of a dancer in flight; the ecstasy of hearing a song you love, sung loud; the smell of dough rising in an oven; a bud pushing through soil; dancing with abandon; lightning flashing over a sea; and the sweet relief of a hot shower after a cold swim.

. . .

Once, when I was living in America, a women's magazine asked me to name my two greatest possessions. Missing the cue to cite something more glamorous, I said my bicycle and my teapot. The editors cut it out of the piece. Dwelling in hilly Sydney now instead of flat Philadelphia, I don't ride bikes often, but I remain deeply committed to my teapots. At work I have three, of different sizes, in orange and spots and swirls of vivid colors; and another at home with Alice in Wonderland perched on the top. Enjoying a freshly brewed pot of tea on my porch, after a swim or a run, is the best thing on Earth. The sun creeps across my feet, cockatoos sweep overhead, and even my tyrannical fluffy cat lies serene in the sun. We all have these moments, where we are sated by simple pleasures. Luxuriate in them.

CHAPTER 15

Ert, or a Sense of Purpose

I have become increasingly convinced true philosophers don't wear tweed coats; they wear wetsuits. There is something delightful about people who become pleasantly fixated on tiny occupants of corners of the natural world, like octopuses or sea dragons or even sharks. Which is how I found myself hurtling along the roads that run like veins from Hobart into the surrounding country, with marine biologist Lisa-ann Gershwin. She sat at the wheel of her red convertible Mazda, drinking chocolate milk as she navigated the purple-shaded hills, cheerily talking to me about jellyfish. My scarf was whipping in the wind, my legs were toasting under the car heater, and I could not have been happier.

The American-born marine biologist told me about the time she was stung repeatedly by the tiny but extremely venomous Irukandji box jellyfish and survived; her concerns about toxic farmlands in China; her favorite jellyfish, the wart-covered translucent Bazinga, which she discovered and which turned out to be a whole new suborder; her love of the beautifully named "long stringy stingy thingy" (a jellyfish technically called *Apolemia uvaria*); the period when she says she was bullied in her workplace and ended up in a homeless shelter; her struggles with depression; the growing global recognition of her work; how the invasion of Tasmania by crown-of-thorns starfish occurred; and what it meant for her to finally be diagnosed with Asperger's. "I finally found where I fit," she said, "after a lifetime of feeling like I'd parachuted down into medieval Japan!" She is perfectly charming and unaffected.

I had called her one day after hearing her talk on the radio, where she constantly laughed at herself and spoke with a vital passion about her great love, jellyfish. I had asked if she would meet me for a quick coffee while I was in Tasmania for a cultural festival called Dark Mofo; instead, she picked me up in her car, wild-haired with the roof down, ready to whisk me off on an adventure. We drove for about fifty miles to the historic village of Oatlands, built by convicts and once home to the longest serving hangman in the British Empire, Solomon Blay, who dispatched more than two hundred people over fifty-one years, and was shunned as a result.

It was not until her late twenties that Gershwin discovered the passion that would upend her life. While in Los Angeles, she decided to visit an aquarium in San Pedro, where she found herself staring at a tall tank shifting with shapes, and fell in love. White moon jellyfish floated in front of her "like clouds in the sky, motionless with dangling tentacles." She was rapt, and almost hypnotized by a sense of reverent wonder. "They were the most beautiful things I had ever seen and they just captured my heart," she recalled. She volunteered to work there and became a scientist who specializes in jellyfish. As a high school dropout, she had to take "a lot of classes" just to get into college; then, after much more study, she won a full scholarship for a PhD at the University of California in Berkeley and a Fulbright scholarship to come to Australia. She is now one of the foremost jellyfish experts in the world and has discovered more than two hundred species.

"They were magical, these spineless, brainless animals with no visible means of support," she said, laughing. "I have dated some men like that! They are alive but like aliens; there's nothing about them we recognize as alive; it's like, 'Who are you and where did you come from?'"

· · ·

Cuttlefish changed my life in quiet ways, while jellyfish changed Lisa-ann's in spectacular ways. Crunching through a plate of liver pâté on toast, she said she had been searching for "ert"—a term she coined, meaning the opposite of inertia—since she was thirteen, and she had only just worked out what it was: purpose. "I don't think it needs to be jellyfish for everybody, but it is for me," she said in her radio interview. "It's having a purpose. It's finding meaningful employment, it's finding a meaningful hobby that absorbs your fascination to a place where depression just can't get in. It just can't exist when you are in that place. So that's ert. Find something you love."

Gershwin's search reached a climax following a protracted experience of depression after a legal dispute with a former employer, during which she found herself living in a homeless refuge in Launceston. She felt, she told me, "an immense inertia that flattened me and held me down like a steamroller. I imagined that if I could figure out what that 'thing' was, then its opposite would be the thing to release me." She wanted something that would make her vertical when she was flat:

> I look back now and I know that I was suffering from depression. But I didn't know it at the time. I only knew that I would sleep for long hours and not get out of bed for days at a time. I wasn't sad; I was lifeless, flat, gray, numb. I was paralyzed by the enormity of something so much bigger than myself. I was acutely aware that life was passing me by, while I was just trying to organize my thoughts enough to make a quesadilla (it's like an incredibly simple Mexican cheese sandwich: one tortilla, folded in half, with shredded cheese in the middle, microwaved for thirty seconds). Sometimes it took days. So for me, without knowing anything at all about psychology or shrinks or mental illness, I just knew that I had to find a way out of that

place. My search for ert became the thread that defined my teens, twenties, thirties, and forties. It wove through everything. No matter how good, bad, or angsty things got, I had this inner drive to find it that was never very far away.

That inner drive returned on the day she moved out of the shelter. She had settled her case and bought a new house with the proceeds; on the same day, the two-thousand-dollar advance for her book on jellyfish, *Stung!*, was mailed to her refuge. She has never cashed it; she framed it and hung it in her new home.

The secret to ert, she told me later in an email, is different for everyone:

For me, it is a mix of someone or something to love (I'm lucky, I have two: jellyfish and my car!), a purpose (my research and writing), meaningful work (work with the Commonwealth Scientific and Industrial Research Organization, an Australian federal government agency responsible for scientific research, CSIRO), and self-care (my fabulous nails!). These may sound incredibly simplistic or even mundane or shallow to someone with loftier goals, but honestly, I'm as happy as a clam at high tide if I've got those.

A clam at high tide doesn't ask for all that much: water, sand, motion.

...

If we get it right, ert can bookend our days with purpose. So we should search for our own ert. It might not be a tangible object. For many people, it is simply motion. For those of us who have been depressed, anxious, or severely ill, ert could just be being able to stand, walk, and move throughout a day. For others it could be swimming, dancing, running, or walking—all of which help to keep us calm and strong, and combat depression and other ailments, as numerous studies have confirmed. Indeed, the point of ert is momentum. One foot in front of the other. One arm circling after the other. One word tumbling out after the other. Whatever propels you forward.

Michael McCarthy, a British environmentalist and journalist, found ert in butterflies. In his book *The Moth Snowstorm: Nature and Joy*, McCarthy describes the moment when, as a seven-year-old, he fell in love with these delicate creatures. It was in 1954, the year his mother was sent to a mental hospital after her mind "fell apart" and Michael and his brother went to live with their aunt in Merseyside, England. One morning, going out to play, Michael noticed a nearby buddleia tree covered with "jewels as big as my seven-year-old hand, jewels flashing dazzling color combinations. . . . How could there be such living gems?" he wrote. It was at this moment, he writes, when "butterflies entered my soul." Thereafter, "every morning in that hot but fading summer, as my mother suffered silently and my brother cried out, I ran to check on them, never tiring of watching these free-flying spirits with wings as bright as flags."

The butterflies ignited a life's passion. Ever since, McCarthy has spent his life studying and admiring the natural world—birds, insects, and blooms—and now he is lamenting the loss of it. *The Moth Snowstorm* looks at the once-abundant, now-dwindling populations of sparrows, larks, mayflies, and moths, reminding us of a time when night drives meant the thudding of hundreds of moths on windshields and regular stops to scrub away the "astounding richness of life" that smeared your vision. Now, he says, humans are wrecking the Earth and trashing our natural abundance. Just as Rachel Carson and so many others have said, McCarthy insists that if we delight in nature and find joy there, we will not so carelessly plunder, neglect, and destroy it. He calls it "defense through joy." Nature is, after all, "part of our essence—the natural home for our psyches."

Bill Cunningham's ert was fashion; documenting it as a historian, photographer, and connoisseur. When he was four years old his mother beat him for wearing his sister's pretty organdy dress and, he wrote, "threatened every bone in my uninhibited body if I wore girls' clothes again," but his love of women's clothing endured. He did not see himself as a good photographer, he said, as he was not aggressive enough: "I just loved to see wonderfully dressed women, and I still do. That's all there is to it." Celebrities were of no interest unless they were wearing something interesting: His clicking finger was an anointing of sorts.

The attention Bill paid to the world, Hilton Als wrote, was a kind of "spiritual practice . . . a loving discipline." A phosphorescence. Als put it simply: "The light that lit Bill from within—his heart light—was that of a person who couldn't believe his good fortune: he was alive. And I'm sure Bill knew that part of the privilege of life is our ability to have hope, that which is the backbone of all days."

American chef Julia Child's ert was, of course, food. Her advice for people was to "find something you're passionate about and keep tremendously interested in it." The woman known for French cuisine and dogged cheerfulness first experimented with cooking during the Second World War while trying to help the navy find ways to stop sharks from inadvertently triggering underwater explosives: She created a shark repellent that is still in use today. She did not discover her passion until her thirties, though, when a meal of oysters and sole in Rouen, she told *The New York Times*, led to an "opening up of the soul and spirit."

For others, beauty can provide ert—both solace and purpose. My friend Shane Clifton, a gentle theologian with a sharp intellect, reports exactly this. Almost a decade ago, he had an accident that left him a quadriplegic. "For a long time," he says, "I was desperately unhappy. Then, against all expectations, I emerged from the grind of despair. I didn't get better, and will always struggle with the limits, pains, and vulnerabilities of a broken body in a world not yet shaped for disability. Yet, joy snuck up on me."

This joy, he says, came from reading the writings of the likes of Aristotle and Thomas Aquinas on the happiness that comes from living a meaningful life, as well as "the Christian gospel, which speaks with a special clarity when we suffer"; from the love of his family and friends; and from discovering "the potent history and diverse gifts of the disabled community," through which he "came to understand that my weaknesses and failures did not render me powerless, but could become fonts of strength."

Through all of this, Clifton says, the revelation of beauty changed him. The once passionate surfer hated the beach after his accident, as he felt "tormented by waves I could not ride." But one night, years after he had lost the use of his limbs, when he was watching a sunset over Sharkies Beach at Wollongong, he says, "I realized that I felt only wonder at the pink clouds reflecting off the glassy waves. And while the sunset was temporary, I started to notice that the natural and social world could be beautiful and awash with meaning." Now he craves beauty, and draws strength and joy from it—as well as, he says, from expensive whisky and laughter.

Ert can be found in work, too. Work often gets dismissed simply as a distraction from what really matters or as simple slog, but being enveloped in work you enjoy—paid or unpaid—can be hugely satisfying and meaningful. This is especially the case if work is your passion, something you love. British biographer Claire Tomalin told *The Guardian* that when she is upset about something, "I go into my study and work." Her work has sustained her through all of the pain and difficulties her life has brought her at times. One of her children died as a baby, another was born with spina bifida, and her first husband, a reporter (who had cheated on her for years), was killed by a Syrian missile. She raised four children on her own; one of them committed suicide when studying at university. Somehow, throughout it all, Tomalin gained respite by entering into imaginative worlds— the lives of her subjects—and writing. She said that closing the door to her study and entering the world she was writing about, such as Charles Dickens's Victorian London, was like entering into another world so completely it was as though she was "sinking into the mud" of the dirty streets. Writing has often been like that for me, too. Utter absorption and purpose.

Ert is that tiny spark within us that reaches out of the mess of daily life toward what is good, and toward what it is we most crave to be, do, and love. Sometimes, it is simply a drive to survive.

CHAPTER 16

Growing by the
Light of the Moon

The bud seemed to follow the moon, and when the
plants were placed at a window with a western aspect
a fresh movement was seen, and this continued until
the moon disappeared behind the hills.

— FRANK CRISP, *JOURNAL OF*
THE ROYAL MICROSCOPICAL SOCIETY

The moon is usually depicted in the popular imagination
as a cover for mystery and menace: the furtive activities of
the burglar, a cue for the howl of the werewolf. But it does
incalculably more than we realize. Without it, the Earth
would spin faster on its axis, our days would shrink, our tides
would grow weaker, and many creatures of the night—bats,
possums, and university students—would be lost. Some
plants turn to follow the moon, responding to its pale curve
and icy light; scientists talk of "tree tides," or a "leaf tide,"

whereby plants move with the moon just as the sea is pulled by the tides, this great force beyond us drawing waves and leaves in arcs of life.

Some plants even grow by, or respond in different ways to, the light of the moon, a phenomenon known as selentropism. It's an almost invisible movement, happening in the dark, on the quiet: the plants slowly curling in by night, unobserved. Something similar happened to me after I was diagnosed with cancer: When the world grew dark, I furled and I grew. Inevitably, the illness changed me irrevocably. But what I did not expect is that my strength would also inch upward. Quietly, almost imperceptibly, and often in the darkest moments, alone in the wee hours of the night, I developed an enduring determination that took even me by surprise. For most of my life, I had confided all the minutiae, agonies, and triumphs of life to a cadre of close friends, but during this period I drew myself inward and in turn grew calmer.

No doubt this was partly enforced by the suffering. I could barely acknowledge all I might lose or consider a future I was no longer certain of, any sense of abandon now replaced by a sedating caution. I could not comprehend the potential losses and did not want to. I thought of the poet Rainer Maria Rilke, who wrote in 1904, "I don't have much knowledge yet in grief, so this massive darkness makes me small." Just the idea that I might not live to see my children grow into adults still makes me cry—leaving children before they are grown is any parent's worst fear.

Yet, as Oscar Wilde said, "Where there is sorrow, there is holy ground," and he was right, hard as it is to till. Sorrow humbles, flattens, and forces you to acknowledge transience, to find peace with God, or your own spirituality. Jewish author Elie Wiesel, who was imprisoned and sent to Auschwitz when he was only fifteen, told *The Paris Review* that his attraction to mysticism led him to discover that what all religions have in common is suffering: All try to address the basic problem of how to deal with it. Christianity, he said, "is almost solely based on suffering." Psychiatrist Viktor Frankl, also a Holocaust survivor and concentration camp inmate, gained renown for his insistence that "if there is a meaning in life at all, then there must be a meaning in suffering."

. . .

I often wondered what it would be like to have a cancer growing inside your body, to suddenly discover you are carrying something that is eating you away, growing in an ugly, consuming mass in or around your bones or organs; to be blithely stepping through life, unaware that your insides are betraying you. I didn't expect to find out, though, at least not for decades. I have always been healthy and strong; I regularly practice hot yoga and swim more than a mile across a bay teeming with fish near my home in Sydney, all while caring for my two kids, hosting a TV show, and writing columns and books.

But now I know: It felt as if I was carrying a baby. The enormous tumors that had been silently growing inside me suddenly ballooned without warning one weekend, pushing my belly out into an arc. It was so odd; in the months beforehand I'd felt bloated, and my clothes grew snug, but my friends laughed and gently drew my attention to the chocolate I consumed when facing deadlines. I was exhausted, but my doctor put it down to my workload.

Then, one Saturday in June, I was struck with agonizing pain and ended up in hospital. The suspected diagnosis was bad: advanced ovarian cancer. "I have to be frank with you, Julia," my surgeon said when I asked if there was a chance it was benign. "All the signs are that this is very serious."

I spent two weeks waiting for surgery, not knowing if I would live to the end of the year. When I walked, it felt eerily similar to being pregnant: organs cramped, squashed up against one another. When I wasn't concentrating, I was sure I'd feel a kick and my hands would creep to my belly, as though protecting an infant. Then I would remember: It was not a baby; it was a mass the size of a basketball, living in between my belly button and my spine. Soon I was almost waddling with it. A dark, murderous infant. I wasn't sure if I wanted to be operated on or exorcized.

Your world narrows to a slit when facing a diagnosis like that; suddenly very little matters. I told my family and some close friends, then went into lockdown. In some ways, it was like being taken by the "Mind Flayer" on the TV show *Stranger Things*: You inhabit the present world and the "upside down" simultaneously, while a mucinous mass threatens to overtake you, to devour and destroy you. You are reminded of this in flashes of lightning and insight no one else can see. By day, you walk on the earth. At night, you crawl through the underworld.

In the early hours of the morning I would wake gripped with terror and quietly contemplate the prospect of death before I rose to get my son and daughter ready for school. I was buttering sandwiches for their lunches when my surgeon called to tell me it looked as though it had spread to my liver. I bit my lip, sliced the sandwiches in half, and held my children's little hands tightly as we walked down the hill to the local redbrick primary school.

In the days before the operation, I turned off my phone and shut down my computer. I prayed so hard I grew unnaturally calm, as though steadying in the light of the moon. I felt like a flower curling in on itself, bracing, preparing for the night, closing to a quiet stillness.

. . .

It's a peculiar, lonely kind of impotence, a cancer diagnosis. Even if you ran a thousand miles, aced a billion exams, or hit a dozen home runs, nothing could reverse or erase the fact of cancer. Except, maybe, surgery.

The operation lasted five hours. The mass was fully removed, but the procedure was far more complicated than anyone had expected. I was in intensive care for eight days, in a tangle of wires, amid beeping machines, with drains in my lungs and my liver. I was so drugged I was hallucinating—Donna Summer was doing water aerobics in the hall outside, Angelina Jolie kept trying to call me (I screened her), a reggae musician sat mute on the end of my bed, my older brother had three heads, one of my feet kept catching fire, and it rained periodically around my bed.

When I closed my eyes, the room was still vivid to me, but the nurses were all clad in *Downton Abbey* garb, and the walls were draped with velvet. I grew intensely attached to the nurses, grateful for their kindness, and lay wondering if there was a more important job.

I also grew attached to my surgeons, who were pleased to discover that the ovarian tumors—one on each ovary—were not malignant. I didn't have ovarian cancer, but I did have another, rare form of appendiceal cancer, which can recur but is nonaggressive and has a much higher survival rate.

Following my first surgery, I was emboldened by the fact that I slowly grew stronger: After a few months I began to wake without scalding pain, was able to walk upright again and return to work. Since then, though, this cancer has returned twice, and I have had to endure two more surgeries, each more difficult than the last. I wrote the first draft of this book before my third, and finished it in the long, grueling recovery afterward, during which I struggled to see a single star blinking, let alone a universe strung with fairy lights. My hospital ward was hung with jellyfish made out of tinsel at Christmas time, and I stared at them glumly. My friends brought me champagne and salted caramel gelato when I was stuck in the ward for my birthday, but I threw up shortly afterward. After this round, the pain was far more protracted and intense, and I had to fight even harder for my calm, which did gradually, slowly, return.

I am so thankful that I am now clear of cancer. My thrice-cut scar runs the length of my torso; I have tried, as Atticus's poetry advised, to wear my scars like wings, but I feel permanently altered. I dread another surgery. It always feels strange returning to normal life. When I came out of the hospital for the first time, everyone suddenly seemed consumed with irrelevant, foolish, temporal worries. Reading the fine print of your mortality is a great sifter of rubbish. I frowned at the complaints posted on social media when I was recovering—people who had the flu, who were annoyed by politicians or burdened by work, or who were juggling jobs and children. I wanted to scream: "BUT YOU ARE ALIVE! *Alive!*" Each day should be a glory, especially if you are upright and able to move with ease, without pain.

I am still grappling with what all of this means. But during this time, three age-old truths became even more apparent to me.

First, stillness and faith can give you extraordinary strength. Commotion drains. The "brave" warrior talk that so often surrounds cancer rang false to me. I didn't want war, tumult, or battle. Instead, I just prayed to God. And I think what I found is much like what Greek philosophers called ataraxia, a suspended kind of calm in which you can find a surprising strength. One that can be developed quietly, in a world of dark, lit faintly by the moon.

Second, you may find yourself trying to comfort panicked people around you. But those who rally and come to mop your brow when you look like a ghost, try to make you laugh, distract you with silly stories, cook for you—or even fly for twenty hours just to hug you—are companions of the highest order. Your family is everything.

Third, we should not have to retreat to the woods like Henry David Thoreau to "live deliberately." And it would be impossible and frankly exhausting to live each day as if it were your last. But there's something about writing a will in which small children are the main beneficiaries that makes the world stop.

My doctor asked me how I became so calm before my surgeries. I told her: I prayed, locked out negativity and drama; I drew my family and tribe—all big-hearted, pragmatic people—near. I tried to live deliberately.

"Can I just say," she said, "you should do that for the rest of your life."

CHAPTER 17

Lessons on Hope
from the Hanoi Hilton

Variable, and therefore miserable condition of
man! . . . We study health, and we deliberate upon
our meats, and drink, and air, and exercises, and
we hew, and we polish every stone that goes to that
building; and so our health is a long and a regular
work; but in a minute a cannon batters all.
—JOHN DONNE, *DEVOTIONS UPON*
EMERGENT OCCASIONS

What is to give light must endure burning.
—ANTON WILDGANS, *HELLDARK HOUR*

As I write this, I am acutely conscious that it may seem as
though I am suggesting we all Pollyanna our way through
life, always looking for the glad things, the bright parts, the
shiny bits. In truth, life is often ugly and awful, and in the

face of it we can grow small, angry, and obsessed with crumbs. We may end up grieving loss or lying in hospital beds with our fists clenched in fear and anger, enduring the diabolical pairing of pain and impotence. I have had black periods during my illness, mainly when eroded by bodily torment or trapped in my house by my own physical limitations, leading me to withdraw from people I don't want to burden. Recovery can be a long march.

I don't articulate my anxieties much, largely because it generally doesn't help if I do. I favor repression over other techniques of coping, just focusing on putting one foot in front of the other. But when I crack, I crack. My body has betrayed me, and at times the pain has been terrible. I have watched my patience ebb as nurses inserted needles clumsily or tightened blood pressure straps too hard; when I've been woken repeatedly for routine checks from five A.M.; when a physiotherapist left me sitting upright in a chair for hours just two days after surgery that had sliced me in half. (On discovering me doubled over, the pain specialist cried, "Is she a sadist? This isn't a gym, this is a hospital!") I resented being told how to eat, how to breathe, and how to walk. I am not an idiot. I am usually pretty fit and strong. I have finished long and complicated tasks, including books and a PhD, run a newsroom, spoken in front of large crowds, written hundreds of thousands of words, passed difficult exams, worked through the night to meet deadlines.

Still, there is something about a cancer diagnosis that can make people around you treat you like a child. Like the pale young hospital psychologist who sprang an unwanted surprise therapy session on me during a checkup. I had never met her before. When I asked if she followed a cognitive behavioral model, she shook her head: "No, because that is all about recognizing false fears. With people like you, all the things you are most scared of might come true. Your fears are real." Cheers.

What I have had to hold on to is that hope is real, too. My friend Briony kept reminding me of this, and the fact that a resilient, hopeful kind of realism was articulated perfectly by a man who endured seven and a half years of torture.

. . .

It would be difficult to find a human being made of sterner stuff than Admiral Jim Stockdale. His full name is, almost incredibly, James Bond Stockdale, but his brand of heroism was not rooted in retro sexism, toys, and martinis, but broken bones and a Medal of Honor. In 1943, Stockdale entered the U.S. Navy at age nineteen, and became an aviator. He graduated to commanding Fighter Squadron 51 and flying supersonic F-8 Crusaders, first at a naval air station near San Diego, then at sea, from aircraft carriers in the western Pacific. In 1965, he led the first bombing mission over the jade-colored hills of North Vietnam.

Sitting on his bedside table throughout his military career, no matter what he was involved in, were the books, *Enchiridion* and *Discourses*, by the philosopher he admired most, Epictetus, a Roman slave who would go on to be a Greek Stoic philosopher; Xenophon's *Memorabilia*, a collection of Socratic dialogues; and *The Iliad* and *The Odyssey* (Epictetus expected his students to be versed in Homer's plots). By studying Stoicism, Stockdale wrote, he became "a man detached—not aloof but detached—able to throw out the book without the slightest hesitation when it no longer matched the external circumstances." Stoics were familiar with the concept that shit happens. Stockdale quotes Epictetus: "Would you have someone else be sick of a fever now, someone else go on a voyage, someone else die? For it is impossible in such a body as ours, that is, in this universe that envelops us, among these fellow creatures of ours, that such things should not happen, some to one man, some to another."

Around midday on September 9, 1965, when flying not far above the treetops in North Vietnam, Stockdale's small A-4 Skyhawk was hit by enemy fire. He "punched out" and watched his plane land in a rice paddy and burst into flames. In an account written almost thirty years later, he described what he says happened next: "After ejection I had about thirty seconds to make my last statement in freedom before I landed in the main street of a little village right ahead. And so help me, I whispered to myself: 'Five years down there, at least. I'm leaving the world of technology and entering the world of Epictetus.'"

It would be almost eight years before he left.

It seems extraordinary—and quite odd—to think that

while flipping out of a low-flying flaming airplane and grappling for a parachute cord as villagers waited below, a person might consciously welcome a philosophical challenge posed by ancient Stoics. But Stockdale says his mental tools were all sharpened and at the ready. One was the ability to separate the things he could and could not control. The former category included "my opinions, my aims, my aversions, my own grief, my own joy, my judgments, my attitude about what is going on, my own good, and my own evil." The latter were all external and included the highly nebulous concept of "your station in life," which he was about to learn was negligible as he plummeted from being the leader of more than a hundred pilots and a thousand men, along with "all sorts of symbolic status and goodwill," to being an "object of contempt," a criminal. Worse was the realization of the body's fragility, "that you can be reduced by wind and rain and ice and seawater or men to a helpless, sobbing wreck—unable to control even your own bowels, in a matter of minutes."

As he floated down, Stockdale could hear shouting below, pistol shots, and the whining of bullets that tore the fabric of his canopy. Then his parachute hooked onto a tree, as a "thundering herd of men ran toward him." He landed on the ground, only to be set upon by a gang of ten or fifteen who kicked and punched him until a policeman sporting a pith helmet came and blew his whistle, breaking up the fray. By then, Stockdale's leg had been badly broken.

This greeting was a harbinger of hell to come. Stockdale

was sent to Hỏa Lò Prison, renowned for its barbaric regime. Inmates were beaten and starved; strapped in stocks, leg irons, or near-asphyxiating rope bindings; deprived of natural light by day and darkness at night; fed soup laced with human and animal feces; and made to stand for several days at a time—the aim being to break the prisoners and force them to publicly criticize the United States. The inmates wryly named the jail the Hanoi Hilton, or Heartbreak Hotel.

Stockdale was one of the so-called Alcatraz Gang, leaders of the resistance who learned to communicate with a tapping code and were regarded as the most dangerous and subversive of the American POWs. They were placed in solitary confinement in a facility a mile away from the prison, locked into tiny windowless cells, where lightbulbs burned around the clock, and made to wear leg irons for pajamas—in Stockdale's case, for two years, half of his stay. The cells burned in the heat, and stank of excrement. One POW died there.

Stockdale scorned his captors. He resisted interrogation and, when told he was going to be paraded for propaganda purposes, disfigured his own scalp, slicing through it with a razor. After his guards said they would cover his wounds with a hat, he beat his face to an unrecognizable pulp with a mahogany stool. When he learned he was going to feature in a film instead, in which he was to tell his fellow prisoners to cooperate with their captors, he tried to kill himself with glass from a broken window. The film was never made. After Stockdale's bloody spectacle, the commissar was sacked and the worst of the torture methods—the ropings—ended. "From then on," Stockdale wrote, "the life was never the same. It wasn't happy, but I shut down that torture system and they never wanted it brought up again."

Finally, 2,714 days after entering the Hanoi Hilton, Stockdale was released. When the POWs came home, he was the first man to limp off the aircraft, to loud cheers. He went on to run for office (in 1992 as a vice-presidential candidate on a ticket with Ross Perot), just like his best friend and fellow Hanoi Hilton sufferer, future senator (and 2008 presidential candidate) John McCain.

. . .

One thing that puzzled onlookers about the story of the occupants of the Hanoi Hilton was how these men who returned with shaded eyes, pasty skin, and stiff limbs become so resilient. How did they cope? How do any of us cope with grueling pain, with devastating diagnoses, with trauma and grief and abandonment, with betrayal and loss and the sheer horror, sometimes, of being a vulnerable spirit housed in a human body? Stockdale's endurance was not simply about detachment, but about hope. He told author James C. Collins that he had survived because "I never lost faith in the end of the story, I never doubted not only that I would get out, but also that I would prevail in the end and turn the experience into the defining event of my life, which, in retrospect, I would not trade." But nor did he kid himself. It was the unrealistic optimists, he said, who did not make it out of Vietnam. "Oh, they were the ones who said, 'We're going to be out by Christmas.' And Christmas would come, and Christmas would go. Then they'd say, 'We're going to be out by Easter.' And Easter would come, and Easter would go. And then Thanksgiving, and then it would be Christmas again. And they died of a broken heart."

Optimism, he was saying, had to be twinned with a tough-minded, open-eyed sense. He told Collins: "This is a very important lesson. You must never confuse faith that you will prevail in the end—which you can never afford to lose—with the discipline to confront the most brutal facts of your current reality, whatever they might be." Collins called this the Stockdale Paradox: a faith you cannot afford to lose, in the thick of whatever you are fighting. Something the Vietnamese would surely have struggled to keep after millions of military and civilian deaths decimated their country.

. . .

I don't believe that every time we fall ill or stumble, we are fighting battles, nor do I like the language that suggests so. But I know what bodily warfare is. And I know what it means to be entirely cognizant of the riskiness and danger of the situation you are in, while simultaneously aware there is also a chance you might yet survive it. I also know how hard and important it is to do as Wendell Berry said: "Be joyful even though you have considered all the facts."

"Yes, the worst might happen," my friend Briony said to me when I lapsed into worrying about the future one day, while watching my dog Charlie bounce on a lush green hill pocked with rabbit holes, "but it might not."

...

When Thomas Merton was living as a Trappist monk at the Abbey of Gethsemani in Kentucky in the 1940s, he was briefly allocated a cell with a tiny window, through which he observed the world. The Catholic mystic and poet wrote:

> God talks in the trees. There is a wind, so that it is cool to sit outside. This morning at four o'clock in the clean dawn sky there were some special clouds in the west over the woods, with a very perfect and delicate pink, against deep blue. A hawk was wheeling over the trees.
>
> Every minute life begins over again. Amen.

CHAPTER 18

Raiding the Unspeakable

Do justice. Love mercy. Walk humbly.

— MICAH 6:8

George Coker, who was a prisoner of war in Hỏa Lò like
James Stockdale, was once asked by a journalist what had
kept him sane during the two months when he was made to
stand still against a wall with his hands above his head every
day from 5:30 A.M. to 10:00 P.M. He said he built houses
from scratch in his mind, designed menus, and prayed repeatedly, by rote. Decades after his release, signs of PTSD
remained: His wife told a reporter from *The Virginian-Pilot*
she would wake at night to see Coker mumbling and shifting, holding his hands over his head: "In his sleep, he holds
up 'the wall.'" His faith had kept him alive, he said, noting
that religion is a "very, very powerful thing. . . . Realizing
there's something better or bigger than just yourself. . . .

That was real for us." But, as Coker told the journalist, he didn't want to be "preachy about it."

Nor do I. I am deeply uncomfortable with preachiness. But I have thought about this a lot, and I think there are a few reasons why people like Coker, and me, find solace in knowing there is something much bigger than all of us, something that we may see "only through a glass darkly," something that we may not entirely understand, that we may often doubt, that may be more easily found in thunderous surf than any religious institution, but something that we often instinctively reach for. Something that can provide a wick for an inner light.

After all, faith and power rarely mix well. Jesus did not come to Earth and tell church leaders to amass large followings, obtain corporate sponsorship and political influence; instead he called those who parroted laws without practicing love vipers and hypocrites. He condemned leaders who were hypocritical and power hungry. He dined with sex workers, not CEOs. As American author Rachel Held Evans put it so well, "The kingdom, Jesus taught . . . belongs to the poor, the meek, the peacemakers, the merciful, and those who hunger and thirst for God. It advances not through power and might, but through missions of mercy, kindness, and humility. . . . The rich don't usually get it, Jesus said, but children always do. This is a kingdom whose savior arrives not on a warhorse, but a donkey."

If I could advise church leaders, I would tell them to stop lecturing about sin, relax their defensive crouch, and just listen for a decade, or a century. Then once they have actually heard and understood, roll up their sleeves and get on with loving people. Then, just listen. The damage of the child sexual abuse scandals and revelations of hidden domestic violence in faith communities has caused a deep and rational cynicism about the church, as have the intolerance of and ignorance about the LGBTQI community and complicity in the colonization and exclusion of Indigenous people. Leaders have been, at best, slow to understand that the church must be a sanctuary for the abused, not a refuge for abusers. At worst, they have perpetrated, condoned, and ignored abuse (both systemic and individual), further traumatizing victims whose lives have been burnt to a cinder by rapists and pedophiles. As written in John 3:20: "Everyone who does evil hates the light, and will not come into the light for fear that their deeds will be exposed."

According to the Bible, God *is* light, the ultimate source of phosphorescence, the light we can absorb to later emit:

God said "Let there be light, and there was light." (Genesis 1:3)

Your word is a lamp for my feet, a light on my path. (Psalm 119:105)

The people living in darkness have seen a great light; on those living in the land of the shadow of death a light has dawned. (Matthew 4:16)

I am the light of the world. (John 8:12)

The light shines in the darkness, and the darkness has not overcome it. (John 1:5)

Light is sweet, and it pleases the eye to see the sun. (Ecclesiastes 11:7)

So, how do we find this light when public debates about belief—and freedom of religion—often contain demeaning, even hateful remarks about the marginalized? It is not easy, especially for women, or members of the LGBTQI community, to maintain something resembling faith in the midst of ugly politicking and hateful sentiments. It makes belief seem bleak and oppressive, neither liberating nor a source of quiet strength and joy. So many Christians are judgmental or incoherent, so many leaders unbendingly uncomprehending or hostile to views different from their own and unwilling to recognize the ways in which the institutional power of the church can be destructive. And yet so many people of faith, like my mother, just quietly shine and care for those around them.

In America, two-thirds of the country still identifies as Christian, though the numbers are in decline; interest in spiritual practices like meditation and yoga has been sharply increasing. According to Pew Research, 22 percent of Americans said they had no religion in the late 2010s, up from

7 percent in the late 1970s, but were "more likely to report feeling a deep sense of spiritual peace and well-being or a sense of wonder about the universe than they were a few years earlier."

So abandonment of the church does not necessarily mean total abandonment of faith. A national study of religion in Australia published in 2017 found that two in three people identify as spiritual or religious. Those who don't identify as such say, "The greatest attraction to investigating spirituality and religion is observing people who live out a genuine faith." One of the times this is most obvious, oddly enough, is at a funeral.

. . .

My great-aunt's funeral was a quiet affair, with just a handful of people scattered across several pews. The priest whose church she attended for decades struggled to do her justice, and seemed to barely know her.

"She was," he said, clearing his throat and looking around, "very good at folding napkins."

This was followed by a long pause.

We don't mark death very well in the West. We so often wrestle the most wretched events into neat formulaic moments: a homily, a hymn, a tearful speech, sometimes not even that. And yet a funeral can be a magnificent occasion, properly done. It should be at exactly these moments that we assess what matters, and what we want our lives to mean, and see, in sharp relief, everything that is puff or nonsense.

One fine example was the funeral held in Redfern for a dear friend of mine, Bishop John McIntyre, the rector of the Anglican parish of St. Savior's. His service was crammed with red-eyed mourners: mothers with babies, collared priests, gay couples, Aboriginals and Torres Strait Islanders, and archbishops squashed next to men in rags. Outside, we were asked to donate money to the Indigenous ministry. Inside, the glass windows were stained yellow, red, and black.

John led a remarkable life. Not just because he was on the fringes of the archconservative Sydney diocese due to his progressive views, but also because he ended up a bishop in Gippsland, Victoria, where he was celebrated for the same views. He was remarkable also because he was a priest who fought for the disadvantaged, the marginalized, and the spurned. He devoted his bishop's stipend to hiring Indigenous ministers. He argued bluntly for the ordination of women in the conservative Sydney synod and laughed off his ensuing pariah status. He instinctively stood with people who were alienated and spat on.

When the church hierarchy condemned him for appointing an openly gay priest to a local parish, he became an "accidental activist," as he said, for the LGBTQI community. He went on to argue for equality and inclusion in his address to the Gippsland synod in 2012. "We now all know that same-sex-attracted people are not heterosexual people who have made a perverse choice about how they express their sexuality," he said. "They simply are what they are."

We don't hear about people like McIntyre much—those who, as his friend the Reverend Bill Lawton put it, "live the art of gentle persuasion." We hear about those who joust with politicians, who use religion for conservative causes, particularly to do with sex and morality instead of poverty, kindness, and justice.

Challenging disadvantage was not a marginal issue for McIntyre, but core to his belief. Pastor Ray Minniecon, who spoke at the funeral on behalf of Australia's Aboriginal and Torres Strait Islander people, said: "He didn't patronize my people or me. He treated me as an equal. . . . He took a special interest in the needs and concerns of the marginalized, the outcasts, the unwanted, and the shut-ins as he walked in and among the community he was called to serve."

Christianity is at its most powerful when it is at the margins, or periphery, not the center of power, and when it is identified with outsiders, not exclusive clubs, and with action, not finger-wagging. As Minniecon said, McIntyre "knew how to put his faith into overalls."

. . .

My own faith is stubbornly cheerful and enduring. I can't quite explain why, but it's untroubled by dogma. I love the mystery, the poetry, even the uncertainty of religion. Stag fights between atheists and religious scholars bore me: They're usually abstract, riddled with clichés, and run by men. My faith is rooted in joy, and confirmed by love and lived experience. It's like the bluebird that Charles Bukowski harbors in his heart, which he writes of in the poem "Bluebird"; though he stifles it and refuses to let it out, he makes a "secret pact" with it that it can sing a little, just "enough to make a man weep."

My faith has endured despite all the rubbish I've heard about women and my queer friends, despite all of the hate mail and insulting messages I have received from conservative Christians who despise my feminism. My faith continues to exist because I have an understanding of humanity as screwed up, of male-led institutions as narrow—blinded by misogyny and sometimes very dangerous for the vulnerable—and a sense of God as large, expansive, forgiving, infinite, and both incomprehensible and intimate.

The older I have become, the quieter my faith has become. It is a great stretching for silence, a reaching for goodness, a resting in a peace that "passes all understanding." A desire to learn how to love better in the face of my countless flaws and constant stuff-ups. A desire to do justice, to love mercy, to walk humbly. A desire many atheists, Muslims, agnostics, Hindus, Jews, Sikhs, Muslims, Buddhists, and others share. We're all on this mad Earth together, bumbling about, trying to figure it out. There is so much we do not know. My problem with many church leaders is that

they too often exclude and judge, defend harmful manifes-
tations of patriarchy, complicate God, and make the expression of faith more like digging a trench than laying down, or
opening, arms.

When I left the fundamentalist churches I grew up in, I
immediately gravitated to one in the red-light district of
Kings Cross, Sydney, led by the Reverend Bill Lawton. He
was a literary-minded man who had been ostracized by his
Sydney peers because he saw women as equals of men.
Women flocked to his parish, along with others who lived
on the streets and on the periphery of the city, vagabonds
and creatives, misfits who thirsted for teaching free of prejudice and full of insight, justice, and poetry. Everyone was
welcomed, without judgment.

To my delight, Helen Garner, the finest writer of her
generation, also regularly appeared in the front pews. I was
in awe of her. I had bought her first book, *Monkey Grip*, in
a garage sale when I was twenty: I started it when I came
home from a party late one night, and finished it as the sky
was growing light, teapot cold on my table. I closed the
book, stood up, showered and dressed, then drove directly
to the library, where I borrowed every book she had ever
written. The next few days were a blur; I gulped her superb
writing down with such greed I lost my sense of time.

So when I saw her small figure at the morning service,
head bent, scribbling in her journal, I tried not to stare. I
understood why she was there, though. Bill was an original

and increasingly radical thinker, and a gifted speaker who preached without notes. As he spoke, homeless people would wander in and out of the service; one roguish gent would occasionally line up for communion, take the full goblet of wine, then make a run for it, spilling red as he sprinted out the front door.

Garner writes lightly about faith. One of my favorite essays of hers is about her friendship with another laconic, gifted writer, like her a Christian drawn more to decency than dogma, Tim Winton. In it, she writes about an incident in the mid-1980s when her born-again Christian housemate was salivating about the prospect of Winton coming to stay: "The saved one was very keen to meet Tim, and had planned a weighty theological discussion: The big black Bible was on the dining room table when we drank our tea and ate our cake. I couldn't face it, and went for a walk around the big park. When I got home an hour later, Tim and the Bible were still at the table." The housemate had gone up for a nap. Winton explained to Garner, "We talked. And in the end I said to him, 'Why don't you give the book a rest? Why don't you let your life be your witness?'"

Let your life be your witness.

In 2017, I emailed Helen when I was in Melbourne for the writers festival to see if she would like to go to a local church. She wrote back excitedly, claiming it was like being invited to a cocktail party. She picked me up at seven sharp outside my hotel, screeching into the curb and apologizing profusely: "I am not used to driving in the city."

We crept into the side chapel where an early communion service was being held for a handful of people. A woman with ginger hair walked in after us with a dog in a ginger coat, soon followed by another dog who sat next to the organ, closed his eyes, and ignored everyone.

There was a rainbow heart outside the church, and as this took place during the heated, often brutal months before the country voted in the marriage-equality nonbinding referendum, the minister prayed fervently for those hurt by current political debates. He spoke of Christ modeling both humanity and divinity, of the fact that suffering is built into being human. Next to me a woman with a silver crutch helped a woman with a walker into her chair. Pegged onto the frame was a note that read WARNING: I HAVE LOW VISION.

Afterward we walked to a coffee shop, where we ate croissants and spoke for three hours without pause. And in between talk of words and books and loves and children and grandchildren and bloody men and the fraught nature of marriage, we spoke of religion, and having a quiet faith. I told her many church leaders had publicly attacked me because of my reporting on domestic violence in the church, and had been sidetracked by a nonsensical debate about statistics that didn't exist. She shook her head: "They think of faith as an argument."

She fell silent for a little while, staring into air. Then she asked, "What is a blessing, do you think?"

"It is a reminder of the divine, and the divine in you. What do *you* think?"

She replied, "It is about a mother and a child." She spoke of the hymn lines where we are told to "look full" in Jesus's "wonderful face," and said that was how a child must feel looking up at its mother. The light of that.

"Yes," I say, "and that means you are lit up, too."

"Yes, I think that's right," she said.

. . .

Faith may be a form of living light, but it is not neat and ordered. It exists in mess and chaos and doubt and broken-ness. Which is something I have learned from one of my favorite priests and thinkers, Nadia Bolz-Weber. She is six foot something, a heavily tattooed former wrestler who knows how to, as she puts it, find God in all the wrong peo-ple. She is an extremely talented Lutheran preacher—perhaps partly because she was a stand-up comedian—who swears by poetry and established a flourishing "misfit" con-gregation in Denver, Colorado, called the House of All Sin-ners and Saints. After exchanging tweets and emails for a couple of years, we finally met in Sydney one day. I picked her up at the airport and drove through thick traffic to Bondi, where we walked along the beach as the moon rose, eating gelato. She was then working on her new book about sex, *Shameless: A Sexual Reformation.* I adored her, and her open warmth and brilliance.

Nadia's faith is rooted in humility. Her most common

prayer, she says, is "God, please help me not be an asshole." Her starting point is that we are all vulnerable and flawed. We have to learn to trust, she writes, that "God makes beautiful things out of even my own shit." The greatest spiritual practice, she says, is "just showing up," being present and attentive.

She is constantly questioning the association of Christianity with the wealthy, the conventional, and the powerful:

> I've never fully understood how Christianity became quite so tame and respectable, given its origins among drunkards, prostitutes, and tax collectors. . . . Jesus could have hung out in the high-end religious scene of his day, but instead he scoffed at all that, choosing instead to laugh at the powerful, befriend whores, kiss sinners, and eat with all the wrong people. He spent his time with people for whom life was not easy. And there, amid those who were suffering, he was the embodiment of perfect love.

Jesus didn't just hang out with the wrong people, he also sent them out as his messengers. As Nadia writes, "Never once did Jesus scan the room for the best example of holy living and send that person out to tell others about him. He always sent stumblers and sinners. I find that comforting."

. . .

The church needs to return to its core business: preaching and practicing a gospel of love. When we are absorbed only with morality debates, we forget what a close community a church can be, and what comfort it can provide. My local church runs a soup kitchen and an outreach for the homeless and victims of domestic violence, and circles those in need with food, presence, and company. For the aging, the ailing, the lonely, and the young, these communities are crucial. The giving of this kind of love is not in any way limited to the church, but it is frequently concentrated there. We lose something important when these communities dwindle and disappear. Many parishioners act as quiet vigilantes of grace, caring for the neglected, the wounded, the lonely, and the needy. My mother sits on the end of a pew in a wheelchair these days; communion is brought to her as grape juice in a tiny plastic cup. I watch the face of the minister—with whom I have some strong theological disagreements—as he leans down to whisper the sacraments in her ear, and am often struck by how gentle he is with her.

Growing up in faith communities, even those that eventually suffocate you, can still bring good things. Tim Winton echoed much of my own experience when he wrote in *The Boy Behind the Curtain* about growing up in a fundamentalist evangelical community, where he initially found joy. He loved singing the rousing hymns—"a rowling mawl of choruses that salved the troubled spirit, like a musical rubdown"—the stories of scripture that were his "imaginative bread and butter," the immediate power of metaphor, the days spent crunching "ethical and cosmic dilemmas," the fascination with some of the lyrical talks that "featured tales of degradation and courage [and] moments of searing illumination."

Church was his "introduction to conscious living": "Nowhere else was I exposed to the kind of self-examination and reflective discipline that the faith of my childhood required. I'd be surprised if anyone at my boyhood church had even read a page of Tolstoy, but it seems to me that the question that ate at him so late in his life was the central issue for us too. What then must we do? . . . We were reaching beyond the ordinary." That's what I believed, too.

Winton learned what a civil life was, how to cultivate disinterest and eschew tribalism in what was a coherent, close-knit, energetic community. They were "doers," he says. "If we stood for anything it was 'love with its sleeves rolled up.'" But, over time, those who questioned were shunned and ousted, and teenagers bursting with thought and questions and ripeness were told to only receive, not dissect, knowledge. Many conservative churches are polluted with a pervasive siege mentality that can lead to a stifling anti-intellectualism and, as Winton puts it, a belief that "a spirit of inquiry was a threat to moral hygiene."

A certain sturdiness can, however, come from spending years developing a daily practice of quiet and prayer; of meditating on how to love, how to forgive, how to be stronger and calmer, how to interpret ancient writings in a modern world; and respecting that there is a spiritual dimension to life, which I see so clearly now in our yearning for awe and an understanding of our own smallness.

At the Brisbane Writers Festival in 2012, Germaine Greer dismissed the Bible as a "silly" book, a "grand delusion," but added that as literature it was a testament to yearning—if you didn't read it you would "not know how strong human yearning is for God, social justice, peace and transcendence."

...

Faith can be an enormous comfort, and prayer a buttress of calm. Researchers have found that a wide array of health benefits result from belonging to faith communities. Even if you don't fit in, or don't want to, there will always be pockets of the world, and various communities, where you can find kindred spirits with whom you can discuss the ancient paths and what it means to ache when you look at thousands of undimmed stars, how to find grace, and if it is even possible to "be still and know that I am God." (The shame is that it is much harder to find those communities if you are a woman or if you are LGBTQI, something the church will need to reckon with in decades to come given the pain this can cause.)

Theology is much like space travel: a wondering about the infinite. The British priest and columnist Giles Fraser once told *The Guardian*: "I think what you have with Christianity is a sense that there is something more, something still to be discovered." Fraser went on to say, adopting the words of Thomas Merton, that theology is about " 'making raids on the unspeakable.' Poetry does it, great music does it, and I think theology is of that order. It's not an attempt to describe the world in a scientific way. It's puzzling over the nature of things." This sums it up so well for me: a puzzling over the nature of things, and a love of nature itself, which is where God is best found. Sometimes the only place. In the sea, the stones, the silence.

Faith is raiding the unspeakable. Grace is forgiving the undeserving. It's a kind of unfathomable magic. And despite everything, if you can somehow try to let your life be your witness to whatever it is you believe, grace will always leak through the cracks.

CHAPTER 19

Embracing Doubt

Certainty is so often overrated. This is especially the case when it comes to faith, or other imponderables.

When the Most Reverend Justin Welby, the archbishop of Canterbury, said recently that at times he questioned if God was really there, much of the reaction was predictably juvenile: Even God's earthly emissary isn't sure if the whole thing is a fiction! The *International Business Times* called it "the doubt of the century"; Archbishop Welby's admission had not just "raised a few eyebrows," it declared, but "sparked concerns if the leader of the Church of England would one day renounce Christianity or spirituality as a whole." Another journalist wrote excitedly, "Atheism is on the rise and it appears as though even those at the top of the church are beginning to have doubts."

Despite the alarm, the archbishop's remarks were in fact rather tame. He'd told an audience at Bristol Cathedral that there were moments when he wondered, "Is there a God?

Where is God?" Then, asked specifically if he harbored doubts, he responded, "It is a really good question. . . . The other day I was praying over something as I was running, and I ended up saying to God, 'Look, this is all very well, but isn't it about time you did something, if you're there?' Which is probably not what the archbishop of Canterbury should say."

Nevertheless, the London-based Muslim scholar Mufti Abdur-Rahman went straight to Twitter: "I cannot believe this." Australian atheist columnist—and my dear friend— Peter FitzSimons tweeted, "VICTORY!" *The Daily Show* account joked, "Archbishop of Canterbury admits doubts about existence of God. Adds: 'But atheism doesn't pay them bills, sooo . . .'"

But Archbishop Welby's candor only makes him human. He may lead eighty million Anglicans worldwide, but he is also a man who knows anguish, rage, incomprehension, and the cold bareness of grief. He lost his firstborn child, Johanna, in a car accident in 1983 when she was just seven months old, and suffered "utter agony." As a teenager he cared for an alcoholic father. When explaining his thoughts on doubt, he referred to the mournful Psalm 88, which describes the despair of a man who has lost all of his friends and cries out, "Why, Lord, do you reject me and hide your face from me?" The psalm also states bleakly: "Darkness is my closest friend."

Faith cannot block out darkness, or doubt. When on the cross, Jesus did not cry out "Here I come!" but "My God, why have you forsaken me?" His disciples brimmed with doubts and misgivings.

Just as courage means persisting in the face of fear, so faith means persisting in the presence of doubt. Faith then becomes a commitment, a practice and a pact that is usually sustained by belief. But doubt is not just a roiling, or a vulnerability; it can also be a strength. Doubt acknowledges our own limitations and confirms—or challenges—fundamental beliefs; it is not a detractor from belief but a crucial part of it.

As Christopher Lane argued in *The Age of Doubt*, the explosion of questioning among thinkers in the Victorian era transformed the idea of doubt from a sin or lapse to necessary exploration. Many influential Christian writers, including Calvin and C. S. Lewis, have acknowledged times of uncertainty. The Southern U.S. writer Flannery O'Connor said there was "no suffering greater than what is caused by the doubts of those who want to believe," but for her, these torments were "the process by which faith is deepened."

Mother Teresa, too, startled the world when her posthumous diaries revealed that she was tormented by a continual gloom and aching to see, or sense, God. In 1953 she wrote, "Please pray specially for me that I may not spoil His work and that Our Lord may show Himself—for there is such terrible darkness within me, as if everything was dead. It has been like this more or less from the time I started 'the work.'" Yet, through this work, she helped many thousands of people.

Some live quite contentedly with a patchwork of doubt: It is not always torment. Who can possibly hope to understand everything, and to have exhaustively researched all areas of uncertainty? How can we jam the infinite and contain it in our tiny brains? This is why there can be so much comfort in mystery.

Just over a month before he died, Benjamin Franklin wrote that he thought the "System of morals" and the religion of Jesus of Nazareth were the "best the World ever saw." Yet Franklin said he had, along "with most of the present Dissenters in England, some Doubts as to his Divinity: tho' it is a Question I do not dogmatise upon, having never studied it, and think it needless to busy myself with it now, when I expect soon an opportunity of knowing the truth with less trouble." A logical pragmatism.

If we don't accept both the commonality and importance of doubt, we don't allow for the possibility of mistakes or misjudgments. While certainty frequently calcifies into rigidity, intolerance, and self-righteousness, doubt can deepen, clarify, and explain. This is a subject broader than belief in God. The philosopher Bertrand Russell put it best. The whole problem with the world, he wrote, is that "the stupid are cocksure while the intelligent are full of doubt."

Of course, doubt goes far beyond the existence of God to the existence of anything and everything. Intellectual rebellion, air for unorthodoxy, and robust questioning should all be part of any open society; and in an era of eroded trust and untrammeled and unapologetic lie telling, the need for vigorous skepticism becomes even more crucial. This is especially the case for science. My friend Dr. Darren Saunders— cancer biologist and associate professor of medicine at the University of New South Wales—said the biggest lesson he got from finishing his PhD was to "embrace doubt, and see shades of gray instead of black and white." Scientists have often been wrong in the past, as have politicians, teachers, priests, principals, CEOs, and all sorts of other authority figures, let alone pundits and bloviators whose work in recent years has been marked by a series of poor election predictions. Think of all the stupid things you have been told over time, by a host of misguided fools and well-meaning people. (Although, seriously, if you can't accept what the vast majority of scientists have to say about climate change, it's not "doubt" that is your problem.)

We should also regularly doubt ourselves, and question what has shaped our own thinking, what unconscious biases we might harbor, and whether we might be wrong. (And there are few things more likely to aggressively propel doubt, of course, than a horrible accident; a cancer diagnosis; a nonsensical, bitterly cruel tragedy.)

All of us have a limited understanding of most things, most especially of the lived experiences of other people. It seems so obvious to state that men won't understand sexism the way women do, straight people won't fathom homophobia the way gays and lesbians can, and white people are extremely poor judges of what racism is. Much as we might like to fancy ourselves freethinkers, all of us carry our pasts in our opinions: the parents, suburbs, and schools that spawned us; the lessons we were taught that confirmed our conventionality or sparked rebellion. We need to know how much we do not know.

Many of the great thinkers of the Western canon have touted the importance of questioning. If you begin with doubts, you will end with certainties, said Francis Bacon. Or you might, at least. When René Descartes discovered some of his own beliefs were false, he decided to rid himself of all the opinions he had adopted and begin again "the work of building from the foundation." Oliver Wendell Holmes, Jr., an associate justice of the U.S. Supreme Court from 1902 to 1932, who was known as "the Great Dissenter," believed certainty was "illusion." "To have doubted one's own first principles," he said, "is the mark of a civilized man."

The mark of a civilized woman, too, is to doubt the wisdom received from men for so long. It's remarkable how ancient and modern texts alike read differently when women have the chance to interpret them. The mark of a civilized person is to recognize that for a long time what we understood to be history—and theology—was history of the few written by the few, and that the voices and experiences of women, the disabled, the poor, the discriminated against, the queer, the black, the colonized, and the "other" have been interpreted by people who never understood what it was like to walk in their shoes, or dance in their bodies, or fight to be free from prejudice. Myths and ideologies have permeated every inch of our written histories, and there is a need for constant rethinking, revisiting, and revision to shed stereotypes of the past and allow a full, bustling, diverse experience of history to be heard. We need to constantly doubt what we are taught and what we read.

And the guiding principle remains the same: When in doubt, reach for experts, as well as those with lived experience, and those who have not been heard; ask whose story and truth is being told; probe the gaps in the evidence; go to original sources; burrow into footnotes; coax the shadows into the light; and perhaps even "follow knowledge like a sinking star, beyond the utmost bound of human thought," as Alfred Tennyson tried to do.

...

"Let your life be your witness." This is the only place of faith I am really comfortable in now, with those who wish to be a quiet witness of love. The egregious sins and stag fights of an institutional church have sullied its public face and caused harm to countless numbers of people; we can too easily forget that the true church is based on love, and lived out in thousands of little parishes, where people care for one another.

Many of us are more comforted by what is unsaid than

said. At the heart of the Christmas story is a baby—God as a naked, poor, newborn refugee; God as utter absence of worldly power. Not a bearded patriarch obsessed with doctrine and church law, but a kid who grew up to teach in parables, then a young revolutionary who was killed for sedition. Who told people to love, to train their hearts to be kind, to let their life be their witness.

Many who don't attend church or adhere to any particular religion congregate on beaches, in forests, and on mountaintops—to experience awe and wonder, to sense a "peace that goes beyond understanding," the "sighs that have no words," and seek ways to bring living light into their lives. Such sites are nature's cathedrals of awe, places where we can sit alongside strangers in silence and understand what we share; where we exclaim at the firefly or the sea sparkles or the cephalopods because they are signs of the miraculous and they usher in a kind of quiet respect for the fantastic, the improbable, and the marvelous, the things we can't quite believe are real, alongside us, here on Earth, where land meets the sea.

Floating in the Bardo

The first, the wildest and the wisest thing I know: that
the soul exists and is built entirely out of attentiveness.
— MARY OLIVER, "LOW TIDE"

In the many months I spent ill and recovering from surgeries, an image kept recurring in my mind: a woman, sub-
merged, under the sea. Not horizontal but vertical, limbs
unmoving, face turned up to the blurred, distant sun.

The sense of being alive but suspended has long encap-
sulated for me a sense of the quiet sacred, of a kind of patient waiting, of a dark peace in the liminal stretch between
the ocean surface and the depths. Where you are alone, but
not afraid.

There, you reach a point of stillness.

I felt like this when I was first pregnant. I would often
duck under the water out past the breaking waves and just

stay there, floating. But it wasn't until I was listening to free diver Michael Adams on the radio that I began to understand why I found comfort there. It was similar to what Tibetans call the Bardo—the transitional state between death and rebirth.

The deeper you go, Adams told radio host Richard Fidler of the Australian Broadcasting Corporation, the more you discard: "The trivia of everyday life falls away. All of the conventional things we waste our time on fall away and I think this is what it is for me, the sense that you are just one tiny speck among all these other living things on the planet. . . . It's very humbling. We put humans on top of the pyramid, we're the boss—[but] down there you're not the boss." It's the smallness of awe: Floating under the surface you compress yourself, you are quiet, tiny in an immense body of water. "It unstitches you in various kinds of ways," Adams said.

He went on to reference Simone Weil, who talked about recognizing the possibility of death that lies locked up in each moment, and he described how "all of us as living things are subject to so much risk and danger on a daily basis. We . . . distance ourselves from that . . . but for most things on the planet life is uncertain and for humans too. And that's what comes into me. That sense of fragility. And it's not frightening, which is the really interesting thing."

Adams does not view time in the depths as similar to the time between life and death, but the time between life and rebirth. Some Buddhist scholars argue this is part of every moment of existence: Every single moment lies between the past and the future.

This is how it feels when you are suspended in the ocean, surrounded by shafts of speckled light reaching down from the surface. The tiny sea creatures lit by these slanted golden columns look like flecks of dust in library light, floating between bookshelves, or fine particles in cathedral light, dancing above the pews.

. . .

In her brilliant Netflix show *Nanette*, Australian comedian Hannah Gadsby spoke about being a lesbian whose favorite sound is that of a teacup sliding onto a saucer and who finds the rainbow flag a bit busy, of her contempt for the misogyny of Picasso, of being raped and assaulted and abused, and of the shame instilled in a teenager growing up in a part of Tasmania where 70 percent of people voted against decriminalizing homosexuality. Stories like hers, she said, as she relived and retold her trauma nightly for months, need to be told. But she said she was done with comedy, done with the kind of self-deprecation that was rooted not in humility but humiliation. The roar of appreciation for her work crescendoed precisely at the moment when she was going to make her exit; the critics spoke in consensus: Her rage, resolve, and candor "broke comedy," broke conventions. Her planned exit became a dramatic reentrance.

Illness breaks bones and thieves organs, but you can rebuild. Staring down death alters you permanently. One of the ways it changed me is that I am now severely impatient with First World problems, with the recurrent complaints of the favored and fortunate, and with the smugness of Instagram posts where people congratulate themselves on their lives and partners and their own faces, rather than looking around them. People complain of such small and stupid things. (One of my American friends assured me that being preoccupied with trivia was a sign of a return to health, and to some extent this is true: I craved lightness and ridiculousness when I clambered back from the underworld of the ill.)

Perspective is a crucial thing. As American author Robert Fulghum wrote, "If you break your neck, if you have nothing to eat, if your house is on fire—then you've got a problem. Everything else is an inconvenience. Life *is* inconvenient. Life *is* lumpy. . . . A lump in the oatmeal, a lump in the throat, and a lump in a breast are not the same kind of lump. One should learn the difference." It's true: We need to resist complaining about experiencing inconvenience. That is what it means to live.

. . .

Sometimes, when infected, wounds can become luminescent. In 1862, during the U.S. Civil War, observers noted that the wounds of some injured soldiers at the Battle of Shiloh began to glow; these wounds healed faster than others. Likewise, in World War I, according to journalist James Byrne, many soldiers had "wounds that glowed in the dark. Not only that, but their fluorescing tissues appeared to heal more cleanly and more quickly than the unilluminated wounds of their counterparts." It seems this effect was caused by a soil-dwelling luminescent bacterium called *Photo-rhabdus luminescens*. But, "naturally, the afflicted soldiers had no idea that the glow was caused by a beneficial bacterial infection and instead interpreted it as the gift of survival from God, handed to them by angels." Hence the name for the phenomenon: "Angel's Glow."

. . .

We are all vulnerable. You realize this when you can no longer pretend you are immortal. Illness can be as random and shocking as lightning. After I wrote a column on cancer for *The New York Times*, I received a call from a man named Jamie Dimon in Manhattan. I was only vaguely aware of who he was, somewhat embarrassingly, but he wanted to talk about my piece, about the idea of living deliberately. The striking CEO and chairman of JPMorgan Chase, who had been listed as one of the world's one hundred most influential people several times by *Time* magazine, told me he had survived throat cancer, and something in my article had struck a chord. He had decided to live deliberately, to focus on family, and cut out superfluous meetings. He was kind, encouraging, and thoughtful. He told me to look him up when I was next in New York.

That Christmas break, I found myself running late to see him, trying to stay calm in a Midtown traffic jam. The cab dropped me on the wrong side of the road and I had to scramble through some bushes in the middle of Park Avenue to get to his offices. When I arrived at JPMorgan Chase, there was a row of security guards with outstretched hands. And then it sank in that Dimon was an emperor of the financial world, with two office blocks filled with New York employees, and an entire floor for his personal staff. We sat in the little room behind his office, which was crammed with photos of his family, and talked about everything that mattered. His eyes welled up when he spoke about telling his daughters he had cancer.

So there we were, a New York billionaire businessman with polished shoes, and a heavily mortgaged Australian writer with twigs still stuck in her hair from crawling through the bushes outside, nodding at each other, understanding entirely what it meant to have your world stripped bare of everything but love and a thirst to survive.

A few months later, when I was back in New York, I emailed him and told him my cancer had recurred. He wrote back quickly, telling me to come to his office so he could give me a hug. Now I see him every time I am in town.

. . .

I wrote this book in the hope that it might be a salve for the weary, as well as a reminder of the mental rafts we can build to keep ourselves afloat, the scraps of beauty that should comfort us, the practices that might sustain us, especially in times of grief, illness, pain, and darkness. I understand, though, that stillness, kindness, the sea, and ancient trees can hardly be a universal panacea for all the suffering on this planet.

There is a lot we don't understand about one another, male, female, and nonbinary; black and brown and white; Indigenous and immigrant; LGBTQI, straight, and cis; able and differently abled, and there are many, many stories we need to hear from people who have been kept down, controlled, silenced, or pushed to the perimeter and locked in there. We are not all equally vulnerable when incarceration, suicide, and mortality rates can be so firmly determined by skin color. I am acutely aware, as Maxine Beneba Clarke, author of *The Hate Race*, pointed out to me, that if she were to write a letter to her children after surviving a lifetime of racist abuse and bullying, in a society where racism is deeply embedded in its systems and institutions, it would be markedly different from my own. With every day we walk on this earth, we must try to understand one another better, and act to ensure that every person can feel fully human, equal, and free. And we must remember what it is we share: that we are born naked and remain naked before fate, which can be cruel and tasteless. But we can also grow by the light of the moon.

And we must remember, too, that even when we are broken, we have a chance to rebuild ourselves anew. There is nothing stronger, Hannah Gadsby said, "than a broken woman who has rebuilt herself." In Japan ceramicists repair broken pottery with gold, silver, or platinum, in a process called *kintsugi* or *kintsukuroi*. They do this to make the fractured object more beautiful than it was before, to honor the cracks and dignify the scars, not hide them. The possibility of death might be locked up in each moment, but so is the possibility of rebirth. Or, at the very least, revamping.

. . .

So what do I know about rebirth or revamping, or about anything? Not much. Lived in a couple of cities, raised a couple of kids, wrote a couple of books, had several surgeries, made a million mistakes. All I offer is some thoughts. And in all of this exploring, I do not entirely agree with T. S. Eliot that we come to the beginning to find ourselves again. After all this exploring, we should be gazing steadily outward, beginning to find others again and the brilliance of the world outside our doors.

What it all comes down to, for me, is attention. Simone Weil wrote that "absolutely unmixed attention is prayer" and she was right. A prayer of care, intent, affection, and presence.

So much of what is broadly called wellness now involves an expensive kind of burrowing into our selves, wobbling on the plank between self-care and self-obsession. Many get lost in the labyrinth of internal observation, an endless cycle of maintenance of muscle, mood, and self-medication.

What is crucial for calm is not just a capacity to empty minds of nonsense but also to fill them with good and marvelous things, with a care for others. There is a reason the great philosophical traditions tell us to cultivate attentiveness to the burdens and struggles of people who live alongside us. The Dalai Lama said: "When tragedy or misfortune comes our way, as they surely must . . . if we can shift our focus away from self and toward others, we experience a freeing effect."

We need to pay attention not just to suffering around us, but to good, and to beauty. (Like my favorite verse in the Bible, Philippians 4:8, says: "Finally, brothers and sisters, whatever is true, whatever is noble, whatever is right, whatever is pure, whatever is lovely, whatever is admirable—if anything is excellent or praiseworthy—think about such things.") What if we can fight distraction not by emptying our minds but by focusing them, so that the mind becomes mind-full, and we find focus, absorption, immersion in something other than ourselves?

Attention is the greatest commodity of the digital age. We pay people to free up our own attention—to freeze our screens, remove our devices, evaporate our clouds, force our heads to focus on the present. We employ people to get us to pay attention to our children, our immediate environment, the trees outside our windows, to our lives, to tell us to stop and breathe, look up not down. We have become toddlers of attention.

We can learn much from artists. After all, what poets and artists, painters and writers, and other creative people do is pay attention. Simone Weil saw paying attention as "the rarest and purest form of generosity"; Iris Murdoch considered it a moral act. The intensely observant Helen Garner is almost rigid with attention. She told Richard Fidler how "intensely interesting" life is, and that observing your surroundings can be an antidote to depression. "How can you not want to be out there among all this stuff? It's so enlivening and moving and funny." It's harder, she says, when you don't care about any of that anymore, when you are trapped in your own head.

Mary Oliver, in her poem "The Summer Day" (aka "The Grasshopper"), observes a grasshopper eating sugar out of her hands, in a moment of serene, acute observation, the kind where the world slows around you as you focus intently on one object. In this moment, she truly sees the grasshopper, masticating and carrying out its ablutions with minute limbs. In doing so, she witnesses something millions would miss. She then writes that while she does not know exactly what a prayer is, she does know how to pay attention:

> Who made the world?
> Who made the swan, and the black bear?
> Who made the grasshopper?
> This grasshopper, I mean—

the one who has flung herself out of the grass,
the one who is eating sugar out of my hand,
who is moving her jaws back and forth instead of
    up and down—
who is gazing around with her enormous and
    complicated eyes.
Now she lifts her pale forearms and thoroughly
    washes her face.
Now she snaps her wings open, and floats away.
I don't know exactly what a prayer is.
I do know how to pay attention, how to fall down
into the grass, how to kneel down in the grass,
how to be idle and blessed, how to stroll through
    the fields,
which is what I have been doing all day.
Tell me, what else should I have done?
Doesn't everything die at last, and too soon?
Tell me, what is it you plan to do
with your one wild and precious life?

• • •

I became obsessed with phosphorescence when writing this book, and became determined to swim in it, or at least see it, somehow hunt it down. It is, however, remarkably hard to observe: You can never predict when it is going to occur in the ocean and it usually lasts only a few hours or days—

despite the fact that, startlingly, three-quarters of all sea creatures have "bioluminescence capability." I packed my wetsuit when I went to Hobart in the hope that my jellyfish-loving friend Lisa-ann Gershwin might be able to show me some hidden spots. She tried, but we had no luck, and stood disconsolately in the dark, throwing pebbles into the sea. All we saw were massive piles of creepy-looking crown-of-thorns starfish, a pest that is thriving in Tasmanian waters and choking parts of the Great Barrier Reef. Lisa-ann came with me to the airport and promised she would call me the very moment she heard of any local occurrences, so that I could drop everything and fly down.

I fruitlessly put a call out on Twitter. I joined Bioluminescence Australia on Facebook and found myself trawling images of glowing ghost mushrooms in remote forests, firefly larvae in Cambodia, and sweeps of neon blue water in Jervis Bay, late into the night. I watched David Attenborough's documentary *Life That Glows* repeatedly. I dreamed of phosphorescence. I longed for it. But I could not find it. The coastlines were quiet.

Then, one day, I was walking down to the ferry, wheeling my bags, on my way to the Garma Festival, in North East Arnhem Land, when I fell into step with a woman called Clair, whose face I recognized from my swimming club. She is part of the tiny group known as "the Crazies" who swim in the dark before dawn, leaving the shore at 5:30 A.M. We grabbed seats on the ferry and she turned to me and said: "It's been incredible this week. There's been this phosphorescence and I have never seen anything like it, even though I've been swimming in the bay for years."

I sat up like a meerkat.

The very first day after my return from Garma, I was down at the surf club at the southern end of Manly Beach blinking in the dark at 5:20 A.M., as Clair and her sister stretched and chatted. Clair brought me a spare light to attach to the back of my goggles. The Crazies all wear them, to stop rogue kayaks from paddling onto their heads; they flash red, green, and white, like Christmas lights.

The sea was black and the sky was black and I felt a little nervous: Sharks feed in the dark. But as we got just a few meters out from the shore, the sparkles appeared. I was transfixed. My fingers threw out fistfuls of sequins with every stroke. A galaxy of stars flew past my goggles. It was as though I were flying through space, like the opening scenes of the *Star Wars* movies, gliding rapidly through a universe only I could see.

We stopped at the point of the headland and looked at one another: We were glowing, lit from beneath, a vivid blue. We laughed, throwing our arms in the air and watching the sequins fall, kicking our feet and creating fluorescent clouds beneath us. I dived down and tunneled through another galaxy, twirling my arms and watching the sparkles follow in the same sweeps and rhythms.

When we got to Shelly Beach we splashed about in the blue-rimmed waves and left twinkling footprints on the sand. As we swam back, the horizon began to slowly burn, and as the sky lightened the sparkles dimmed. We reentered the world, and the lights faded. We walked up the shore, gasping at the sheer beauty, wonder, and miracle of it all.

I floated on air for days and days. I went three more times, and each time was astounded.

And all of this was in the bay at the bottom of my hill.

In a similar way, the answers to the questions that inspired this book—How do we endure when suffering becomes unbearable and our obstacles seem monstrous? How do we continue to glow when the lights turn out?—are there, right in front of us, all the time. All we can do, really, is keep placing one foot on the earth, then the other, to seek out ancient paths and forests, certain in the knowledge that others have endured before us. We must love. And we must look outward and upward at all times, caring for others, seeking wonder and stalking awe, every day, to find the magic that will sustain us and fuel the light within—our own phosphorescence. And we must always, always pay attention to the world as we live our one wild and precious life, even when we're floating in the Bardo, about to return to the surface, bursting for air.

ACKNOWLEDGMENTS

"We are all worms," Winston Churchill reportedly said, "but I do believe that I am a glow-worm." This book has been written with the support of the many glow-worms in my life. First, my Australian publisher, Catherine Milne, whose eyes lit up when I first mentioned this book, and who has championed it tirelessly ever since. My dynamite agent, Binky Urban, whose cool tenacity, instincts, and loyalty are rightfully the stuff of legend. My American publishers, the sagacious and distinguished Kate Medina and the talented Erica Gonzalez from Random House.

I am indebted also to the wonderful Professor Peter Kanowski from University House in Canberra, for allowing me to write in residence for two weeks, in a place so peaceful and quiet, down by the lake, that I experienced alarming bursts of productivity.

I have been toying with, and developing some of, the ideas in this book for years. I have run them up flagpoles with some of my outstanding editors, including Trish Hall and Julie Lewis, and in particular Matt Seaton. Earlier versions, or fragments of, some of these chapters appeared in my columns in *The New York Times*, including "Women, Own Your 'Dr.' Titles," June 28, 2018; "Forget Calories. Exercise for Awe," May 6, 2017; "Don't Dress Your Age," October 21, 2016; "Being Dishonest About Ugliness," November 9, 2015; "Was It Cancer? Getting the Diagnosis," September 2, 2015; "How We Misread Renée's Face," October 28, 2014; and "Doubt as a Sign of Faith," September 25, 2014.

Shorter versions or threads of some of these chapters also appeared in my *Sydney Morning Herald* columns: "What I Really Want to Teach My Son—and What He Is Teaching Me," June 1, 2018; "Christianity Most Powerful at the Margins of Power," June 20, 2014; and "How to Keep a BFF for, Well, Ever," February 1, 2014, as well as on the Australian Broadcasting Corporation's website, abc.net.au, in the article "'It's About Loss': The Transient Beauty of Rone," October 18, 2016. Some portions also appeared in *Newsweek*: "Why We Need Silence (Not Cell Phones)," October 21, 2009, and "America's Vanishing Spaces," January 27, 2010.

I would like to loudly applaud and acknowledge my excellent colleagues at the Australian Broadcasting Corporation, who have tolerated both my absence and my presence, in particular my smart, hardworking team at *The Drum*: Annie White, Emily Smith, Jamie Cummins, Ellen Fanning, Margie Smithurst, Dale Drinkwater, Ghada Ali, Melanie Lobendahn, Lillian Radulova, Sam Bold, and the delightful Steph Boltje. I am grateful for the comradeship of my exceptional work-sister, Hayley Gleeson, and the ongoing encouragement of Tim Ayliffe, Gaven Morris, and Grant Sherlock. I am thankful also to those who read early drafts and provided incisive feedback, including Darren Saunders, Catherine Keenan, Tim Dick, James Woodford, Leigh Sales, Naomi Priest, Martha Sear, and Shane Clifton. Thanks also to Marcia Langton and Ali Alizadeh, who offered thoughts and expertise on particular sections. My Australian editor Scott Forbes's sharp eye and literary insights prodded me repeatedly in a better direction. And Alice Woods's enthusiasm provided a ready propeller in any moments of stasis.

And to all those marvelous people who helped the writing of this book in so many different ways: Candy Royalle, Maureen Dowd, Jamie Dimon, Lisa-ann Gershwin, Richard Fidler, Helen Garner, Nick Dawkins, Paul Austin and Carl Adams, Nadia Bolz-Weber, my writing buddy Jacqui Maley, Annabel Crabb, Lucie Beaman, Mia Freedman, Sacha Molitorisz, Jo Dalton, Joel Gibson, Peter FitzSimons and Lisa Wilkinson, Megan Fraser, Jeremy Travers, Kate Zarifeh, Sarah Steed, Anna Leavy, and all of my mates in Manly's Bold and Beautiful swim squad.

As I mention in this book, I have had some bouts of illness over the past few years. The kindness of those friends who stayed by my side when the world narrowed to a pinpoint meant everything, especially Jo Chichester, Briony

Scott, Caitlin McGee, Cath Keenan, Geoff Broughton, Woody, Zab, Josie Grech, Sarah Macdonald, and Jo Fox. And, of course, Jock: You, my friend, are singular and spectacular.

One significant area I did not cover in this book is family. All of the members of my family have taught me a great deal about inner light. My two brothers, Mike and Steve, to me, exemplify decency. They, along with my sisters-in-law; my nieces, Cate and Laura; and my nephews, Luke, Elijah, Oscar, and Sebastian, are a constant source of love and comedy.

My parents have taught me most of all—my father, about integrity, generosity, speaking your mind, fighting for the vulnerable, and the importance of daily swimming. My mother—a woman who is truly phosphorescent—has taught me about grace, faith, quiet devotion, and a gentle joy. She is the lamp that lit our family, and does still.

My children, Poppy and Sam, turned my heart inside out on the days when they were born. They make me laugh so hard, and I love watching them grow, seeing their brains boggle, crackle, and fire. I feel incredibly lucky to be their mother.

I wrote this book for them—as well as for my beautiful, much-loved godchildren, Archie, Ollie, Hugo, Ava, Saskia, and Florence. All of them have been little glow-worms for me, and will go on to light up the world.

NOTES

ix (Epigraph): As paraphrased by William Luce in his play about Dickinson, *The Belle of Amherst*, which opened in the Longacre Theatre on Broadway in 1976. In the author's note at the front of the printed version of the play, Luce writes that Dickinson's poems and letters "radiate an invisible light." He described the experience of reading them as "much like looking obliquely at a star in order to see it." William Luce, *The Belle of Amherst* (New York: Dramatists Play Services, 2015), 3.

PRELUDE. A Light Within

xvi **"The human body literally glimmers"** Masaki Kobayashi, Daisuke Kikuchi, and Hitoshi Okamura, "Imaging of Ultraweak Spontaneous Photon Emission from Human Body Displaying Diurnal Rhythm," *PLOS One* 4, no. 7 (July 16, 2009): 6256.

xviii **"There had been lots of swell"** Dorothy Freeman and Martha E. Freeman, eds., *Always, Rachel: The Letters of Rachel Carson and Dorothy Freeman, 1952–1964* (Boston: Beacon Press, 1995), 186–87.

xix **"It was one of those experiences"** Ibid.

xx **"the Wheels of Poseidon"** "A History of Bioluminescence According to E. N. Harvey," Scripps Institution of Oceanography, April 14, 2016.

xx **"a sea that presented"** Charles Darwin, *The Voyage of the Beagle* (London: J. M. Dent & Sons, 1936), 496.

xxi **"an easy, simple source of light"** Ferris Jabr, "The Secret History of Bioluminescence," *Hakai Magazine*, May 10, 2016.

xxii **naval officers struggled to describe what they saw** Unless otherwise indicated, the quotes on pages xxii–xxiii are all from Robert F. Staples, *The Distribution and Characteristics of Surface Bioluminescence in the Oceans*, U.S. Naval Oceanographic Office, Washington, D.C., March 1966, apps.dtic.mil/dtic/tr/fulltext/u2/630903.pdf. Staples's seminal study of these "sadly neglected" organisms sold for ninety cents each. He had studied about three thousand reports of lit-up seas, mostly from shipping lanes, as well as British and U.S. naval and coast guard reports and scientific cruise reports.

xxiii **does not appear to have been replicated, either** Jabr, "Secret History of Bioluminescence." This phenomenon, writes Jabr, was described by physician Georg Eberhard Rumphius in the late 1600s.

xxiii **dried fish skins were also unsuccessful** Andrew Watson, "Miners Lamp History from Flame to 'the Davy Lamp' to Electric," *Health and Safety International*, September 2018.

xxiii **replace electricity in a "biobulb"** Rachel Nuwer, "One Day We'll Light Our Homes with Bacteria," Smithsonian .com, August 15, 2013.

xxv **"that kind of happiness"** Quoted in Pico Iyer, "The Joy of Quiet," *The New York Times*, December 29, 2011.

PART I. Awe, Wonder, and Silence

3 **"The most beautiful thing we can experience"** Albert Einstein, *Living Philosophies* (New York: Simon & Schus-

ter, 1931), quoted in David E. Rowe and Robert J. Schulmann, eds., *Einstein on Politics: His Private Thoughts and Public Stands on Nationalism, Zionism, War, Peace, and the Bomb* (Princeton, N.J.: Princeton University Press, 2007), 229.

4 **"when something quite new and singular"** Adam Smith, *The Essential Adam Smith* (New York: W. W. Norton, 1987), 25–26.

4 **"frightened girl"** Oscar Wilde, *The Harlot's House,* quoted in Frank Harris, *Oscar Wilde* (Ware, Hertfordshire, UK: Wordsworth Editions, 2007), 52.

CHAPTER 1. Lessons from a Cuttlefish

7 **"Those who dwell"** Rachel L. Carson, *The Sense of Wonder* (New York: Harper and Row, 1956).

9 **"an octopus attached to a hovercraft"** Peter Godfrey Smith, *Other Minds: The Octopus and the Evolution of Intelligent Life* (London: HarperCollins, 2017), 200.

11 **"experiences of awe bring people"** Melanie Rudd, Kathleen Vohs, and Jennifer Lynn Aaker, "Awe Expands People's Perception of Time, Alters Decision-Making, and Enhances Well-Being," *Psychological Science*, January 1, 2012.

12 **people who regularly feel awe** Paul Piff et al., "Awe, the Small Self, and Prosocial Behavior," *Journal of Personality and Social Psychology* 108, no. 6 (June 2015): 883–99.

13 **water "meditates *you*"** Wallace J. Nichols, *Blue Mind: The Surprising Science That Shows How Being Near, In, On, or Under Water Can Make You Happier, Healthier, More Connected, and Better at What You Do* (New York: Little, Brown, 2014).

13 **in August 2018** Christoffer van Tulleken et al., "Open Water Swimming as a Treatment for Major Depressive Disorder," *BMJ Case Reports*, 2018-225007, August 21, 2018.

13 **"If you adapt to cold water"** Quoted in Layal Liverpool, "Could Cold Water Swimming Help Treat Depression?," *The Guardian*, September 13, 2018.

15 **One of the world's longest studies** Harvard Study of Adult Development, adultdevelopmentstudy.org. See also Robert Waldinger's TED Talk, "What Makes a Good Life? Lessons from the Longest Study on Happiness," November 2015.

15 **than he did previously** Liz Mineo, "Good Genes Are Nice, but Joy Is Better," *The Harvard Gazette*, April 11, 2017.

15 **"social cure"** Alexander K. Saeri et al., "Social Connectedness Improves Public Mental Health: Investigating Bidirectional Relationships in the New Zealand Attitudes and Values Survey," *Australian & New Zealand Journal of Psychiatry*, August 12, 2017.

16 **"weak social ties"** G. M. Sandstrom and E. W. Dunn, "Social Interactions and Well-Being: The Surprising Power of Weak Ties," *Personality and Social Psychology Bulletin* 40, no. 7 (July 2014): 910–92.

19 **"Two appraisals are central"** Dacher Keltner and Jonathan Haidt, "Approaching Awe, a Moral, Spiritual, and Aesthetic Emotion," *Cognition and Emotion*, August 18, 2010, 126.

19 **shadowed by a huge—if extinct—beast** Piff et al., "Awe, the Small Self, and Prosocial Behavior."

19 **"awe produces a vanishing self"** Dacher Keltner in Jo Marchant, "Awesome Awe: The Emotion That Gives Us Superpowers," *New Scientist*, July 26, 2017.

20 **"music played on a street corner"** Emma Stone, "The Emerging Science of Awe and Its Benefits," *Psychology Today*, April 27, 2017.

CHAPTER 2. "A Better Show Outside"

23 **"most beautiful [storm] cell of the decade"** Nick Moir, "'Like Looking at a God': Chasing the Storms Roiling Tornado Alley," *The Sydney Morning Herald*, May 19, 2019.

23 **"makes you feel really small"** Stephen Smit, "Storm Photographer Nick Moir Describes the Beauty of the
Weather," *Vice*, July 27, 2018.

24 **"I felt the full range of emotions from fear to ecstasy"**
Krystle Wright (director), *Chasing Monsters*; film and interview at monsterchildren.com/90056/chasing-storms-for
-a-living-canon-krystle-wright.

24 **"First is the sheer, raw experience"** David Hoadley,
"Commentary: Why Chase Tornadoes?," *Storm Track*,
March 1982, 1.

25 **hunting and photographing severe thunderstorms** Tim
Marshall, "An Evening with Dr. Jensen," *Storm Track*,
November–December 1996, stormtrack.org/library/
archives/20anniv.htm#jensen. Hoadley said it was two
years earlier, in Minnesota, though *Storm Track* said it was
in the late 1940s in the upper Midwest. Jensen himself
said it was summer 1953.

25 **"I hope they are out chasing for the same reasons"** Ibid.

25 **the average age is thirty-five** Roger Edwards and Tim
Vasquez, "The Online Storm Chasing FAQ," *Storm Track*,
August 13, 2002.

26 **"I just noticed a funnel hanging"** "Weather from Hell Is
Heaven on Earth for Storm Troops," *The Age*, July 4, 2004.

28 **"the first satisfactory explanation of rainbows"** A. C. Grayling, "Descartes," *The New York Times*, February 4, 2007.

29 **"one of the defining elements of human spirituality"**
Robert C. Fuller, *Wonder: From Emotion to Spirituality*
(Chapel Hill: University of North Carolina Press, 2006).

29 **"wide-eyed, slack-jawed feeling"** Jesse Prinz, "How Wonder Works," Aeon.co, June 21, 2013.

29 **"most of us walk unseeing through the world"** Rachel Carson, *Silent Spring* (New York: Houghton Mifflin, 1962), 220.

30 **"The Narrative Imagination"** Martha Craven Nussbaum,
*Cultivating Humanity: A Classical Defense of Reform in
Liberal Education* (Cambridge, Mass.: Harvard University
Press, 1997), 89.

30 **"reveal to them an alternative world"** Daniel Burke, "A Rock Star Was Asked What God's Voice Sounds Like. His Answer Is Beautiful," CNN.com, June 30, 2019.

31 **"after a few hours of dejected driving"** David Hoadley profile in *Storm Track* magazine, stormtrack.org.

CHAPTER 3. The Overview Effect

33 **"I realized how insignificant we all are"** "The Earth Behind a Man's Thumb," *Newsweek*, October 11, 2007. Lovell was also struck by the vibrancy of the Earth in contrast to the moon: "The Moon is nothing but shades of gray and darkness. But the Earth—you could see the deep blues of the seas, the whites of the clouds, the salmon pink and brown of the land masses."

33 **"It suddenly struck me"** "Right Here, Right Now," NASA Earth Observatory website, October 2, 2017, earthobservatory.nasa.gov/images/91494/right-here-right-now.

34 **"evangelists, preaching the gospel of orbit"** Christian Davenport and Julie Vitkovskaya, "50 Astronauts, in Their Own Words," *The Washington Post*, June 19, 2019.

34 **renewed faith or on a quest for wisdom** Astronauts have returned as a born-again Christian (Apollo 16's Charlie Duke), a poet (Apollo 14's Al Worden), an evangelist (Apollo 15's Jim Irwin), and a founder of an institute devoted to understanding the science of inner wisdom (Apollo 14's Edgar Mitchell).

34 **send people into virtual space** David B. Yaden et al., "The Overview Effect: Awe and Self-Transcendent Experience in Space Flight," *Psychology of Consciousness: Theory, Research, and Practice* 3, no.1 (2016): 1–11. See also L. Reinerman-Jones and B. Sollinsa, "Neurophenomenology: An Integrated Approach to Exploring Awe and Wonder," *South African Journal of Philosophy* 32, no. 4 (2013): 295–309.

34 **"scars of national boundaries"** Stacy Shaw, "The Overview Effect," *Psychology in Action*, January 1, 2017.

35 **"you feel this incredible connection to the Earth"** Ibid.

35 **"very connected with the rest of the universe"** Mick Brady, "Star Explorer Mae Jamison: The Sky Connects Us," *TechNewsWorld*, November 13, 2018.

35 **"Life is best when you live deeply and look up"** Amy McCaig, "Jemison: 'Life Is Best When You Live Deeply and Look Up,'" Rice University, May 13, 2017.

35 **"the sad beauty of human suffering"** Benito Ortolani, *The Japanese Theatre: From Shamanistic Ritual to Contemporary Pluralism* (Princeton, N.J.: Princeton University Press, 1995), 325.

35 **"To watch the sun sink behind a flower clad hill"** Zeami Motokiyo, quoted by Yury Lobo, *In the Wake of Basho: Bestiary in the Rock Garden*, self-published, 2016.

35 **"an awareness of the universe"** Christopher Chase, "Yugen," Traditional Kyoto, traditionalkyoto.com/culture/yugen/.

36 **Kathryn D. Sullivan . . . was also gobsmacked** Shaw, "Overview Effect."

36 **"stunned in a way that was completely unexpected"** Yasmin Tayag, "Six NASA Astronauts Describe the Moment in Space 'When Everything Changed,'" *Inverse*, March 27, 2018.

37 **"more in touch with humanity"** Richard Feloni, "NASA Astronaut Scott Kelly Explains How Seeing Planet Earth from Space Changed His Perspective on Life," *Business Insider*, February 27, 2018.

37 **"The planet is incredibly beautiful"** Ibid.

38 **can lead people to make smarter global decisions** Chris Hadfield, "How Space Travel Expands Your Mind," bigthink.com, March 23, 2018.

38 **Sagan wrote about the sight of Earth** Carl Sagan, *Pale Blue Dot: A Vision of the Human Future in Space* (New York: Ballantine, 1994).

CHAPTER 4. Nature Deficit Disorder: On Biophilia

40 **"People from a planet without flowers"** Iris Murdoch, *A Fairly Honourable Defeat* (New York: Viking Press, 1970), 162.

41 **Theodore Roosevelt understood** Theodore Roosevelt, "The Words of Theodore Roosevelt: African Game Trails" (Urbana-Champaign: Charles Scribner's Sons, University of Illinois), ix.

41 **"went with being manly"** Jonathan Rosen, "Natural Man," *The New York Times*, August 6, 2009, nytimes.com/2009/08/09/books/review/Rosen-t.html.

42 **"We've got responsibilities"** Florence Williams, *The Nature Fix: Why Nature Makes Us Happier, Healthier, and More Creative* (New York: W. W. Norton, 2017), 4.

42 **have been recognized** Johann Hari, *Lost Connections: Uncovering the Real Causes of Depression—and the Unexpected Solutions* (New York: Bloomsbury, 2018), 126.

42 **"nature deficit disorder"** The term was coined by American writer Richard Louv in his book *Last Child in the Woods: Saving Our Children from Nature Deficit Disorder* (Chapel Hill, N.C.: Algonquin, 2005).

43 **alcohol, cigarettes, and harmful foods** University of Plymouth, "Seeing Greenery Linked to Less Intense and Frequent Unhealthy Cravings," *Science Daily*, July 12, 2019.

43 **from adolescence into adulthood** Kristine Engemann et al., "Residential Green Space in Childhood Is Associated with Lower Risk of Psychiatric Disorders from Adolescence into Adulthood," *Proceedings of the National Academy of Sciences* 116, no. 11 (March 2019): 5188–93.

44 **perform better in tests** Frances E. "Ming" Kuo, "Coping with Poverty: Impacts of Environment and Attention in the Inner City," *Environment & Behavior* 33, no. 1 (2001): 5–34.

44 **those who gazed only at brick walls** E. O. Moore, "A Prison Environment's Effect on Health Care Service De-

mands," *Journal of Environmental Systems* 11 (1981–82): 17–34. See also Howard Frumkin, "Beyond Toxicity: Human Health and the Natural Environment," *American Journal of Preventive Medicine* 20, no. 3 (2001): 237.

44 **"healing gardens"** R. Ulrich, "View Through a Window May Influence Recovery from Surgery," *Science* 224, no. 4647 (April 27, 1984): 420–21.

44 **"improves health perception"** Omid Kardan et al., "Neighborhood Greenspace and Health in a Large Urban Center," *Scientific Reports* 5, no. 11610 (2015).

45 **"to help a passerby than those entering it"** C. Song, H. Ikei, and Y. Miyazaki, "Physiological Effects of Nature Therapy: A Review of the Research in Japan," *International Journal of Environmental Research and Public Health* 13 (2016): 781.

45 **"The more nature, the better you feel"** Williams, *Nature Fix.*

45 **"I have seen, in fevers"** Florence Nightingale, *Notes on Nursing: What It Is and What It Is Not* (London: Harrison, 1860), 83–84.

46 **immerse ourselves in nature** Dr. Qing Li, *Shinrin-Yoku: The Art and Science of Forest-Bathing* (London: Penguin, 2018).

47 **limit, or decrease, rumination** Gregory N. Bratman et al., "Nature Experience Reduces Rumination and Subgenual Prefrontal Cortex Activation," *Proceedings of the National Academy of Sciences of the United States of America* 112, no. 28 (July 14, 2015): 8567–72.

47 **sixty-four studies of forest bathing** Margaret M. Hansen, Reo Jones, and Kirsten Tocchini, "Shinrin-yoku (Forest Bathing) and Nature Therapy: A State-of-the-Art Review," *International Journal of Environmental Research and Public Health* 4 (2017): 851.

47 **a Tokyo study of three thousand people** T. Takano, K. Nakamura, and M. Watanabe, "Urban Residential Environments and Senior Citizens' Longevity in Megacity

Areas: The Importance of Walkable Green Spaces," *Journal of Epidemiology & Community Health* 56, no. 12 (December 2002): 913–18, cited in Frances E. "Ming" Kuo, "Nature-Deficit Disorder: Evidence, Dosage, and Treatment," *Journal of Policy Research in Tourism, Leisure and Events* 5, no. 2 (2013): 172–86.

48 **The authors of the 2017 meta-analysis wrote** Hansen, Jones, and Tocchini, "Shinrin-yoku (Forest Bathing) and Nature Therapy," 43–44.

49 **the sharpest and harshest of urban environments** Kuo, "Nature-Deficit Disorder," 172–86.

50 **though it is not certain why** Bratman et al., "Nature Experience Reduces Rumination": 8567–72.

56 **"therapeutic landscapes"** Quoted in Sarah L. Bell et al., "From Therapeutic Landscapes to Healthy Spaces, Places and Practices: A Scoping Review," *Social Science and Medicine* 196 (2018): 123–30.

56 **chemicals (phytoncides) exuded by trees** Frances E. "Ming" Kuo, "How Might Contact with Nature Promote Human Health? Promising Mechanisms and a Possible Central Pathway," *Frontiers in Psychology*, August 25, 2015: 1093.

56 **"nature helps in every form, and in every dose"** Kuo, "Nature-Deficit Disorder," 178.

58 **"the presence of water generated greater effects"** J. Barton and J. Pretty, "What Is the Best Dose of Nature and Green Exercise for Improving Mental Health? A Multistudy Analysis," *Environmental Science & Technology* 44, no. 10 (May 15, 2010): 3947–55.

58 **A 2016 study** Daniel Nutsford et al., "Residential Exposure to Visible Blue Space (but Not Green Space) Associated with Lower Psychological Distress in a Capital City," *Health & Place*, May 2016, 70–78.

59 **"All sanity depends on this"** Doris Lessing, *The Golden Notebook* (New York: Harper Perennial, 1994), 573.

60 **"country is much more than a place"** Ambelin Kwaymul-

lina, "Seeing the Light: Aboriginal Law, Learning and Sustainable Living in Country," *Indigenous Law Bulletin* 6, no. 11 (May/June 2005).

CHAPTER 5. Why We Need Silence

61 **"Let tiny drops of stillness fall gently through my day"** A reflection by Miriam-Rose Ungunmerr-Baumann, "Dadirri: Inner Deep Listening and Quiet Still Awareness," author's own copy, used with permission.

61 **"the audible expression of all that is exultant"** C. S. Lewis, *Five Best Books in One Volume* (first published in 1969 by Iversen Associates; digitized in 2008 by Indiana University), 80.

62 **"The day will come"** James L. Hildebrand, *Noise Pollution and the Law* (Buffalo, N.Y.: William S. Hein, 1970), 62.

62 **"major breakthrough for the powers of hell"** Sara Maitland, *A Book of Silence* (Berkeley, Calif.: Counterpoint, 2010), 39–40.

63 **"Unnecessary noise"** Nightingale, *Notes on Nursing*, 47.

63 **complete lack of "all audible mechanical vibrations"** See Gordon Hempton and John Grossman, *One Square Inch of Silence: One Man's Search for Natural Silence in a Noisy World* (New York: Simon & Schuster, 2009); Julia Baird, "America's Vanishing Silent Spaces," *Newsweek*, October 27, 2010; and Hempton's website, soundtracker .com.

64 **"Silence is the moonlit song of the coyote"** Hempton and Grossman, *One Square Inch of Silence*, 2–3.

65 **"Besides spending time away"** Baird, "America's Vanishing Silent Spaces."

69 **"*Dadirri* recognizes the deep spring"** Ungunmerr-Baumann, "Dadirri: Inner Deep Listening and Quiet Still Awareness."

PART II. We Are All Wiggly

76 **our lives inevitably arc from good to bad** Dan McAdams, "The Redemptive Self: Generativity and the Stories Americans Live By," *Research in Human Development* 3, nos. 2 and 3 (2006): 81–100.

76 **Psychologists have also long found signs** Christopher Peterson, Martin E. Seligman, and George E. Vaillant, "Pessimistic Explanatory Style Is a Risk Factor for Physical Illness: A Thirty-Five-Year Longitudinal Study," *Journal of Personality and Social Psychology* 55, no. 1 (July 1988): 23–27.

77 **"create a virtuous cycle of care"** Brady K. Jones and Dan P. McAdams, "Becoming Generative: Socializing Influences Recalled in Life Stories in Late Midlife," *Journal of Adult Development* 20, no. 3 (September 2013): 158–72.

77 **"We have, each of us, a life-story"** Oliver Sacks, *The Man Who Mistook His Wife for a Hat and Other Clinical Tales* (London: Simon & Schuster, 1988), 110.

78 **"People are really a slave to winning people's approvals"** Dan Wootton, "Madge's War on Social Media," *The Sun*, June 14, 2019.

78 **"edit their pictures in order for them to look 'perfect' "** Young Health Movement, *#StatusOfMind: Social Media and Young People's Mental Health and Wellbeing*, Royal Society for Public Health, May 2017.

78 **"To be ourselves"** Sacks, *Man Who Mistook His Wife for a Hat*, 111.

78 **no one can make you feel inferior** This quote appears to have been first published in *Reader's Digest* in September 1940. According to the Quote Investigator website, it is likely a synthesis of remarks Eleanor Roosevelt made after being snubbed at an event at the University of California in 1935, when the First Lady defined a snub as "the effort of a person who feels superior to make someone else feel

inferior. To do so, he has to find someone who can be made to feel inferior." See quoteinvestigator .com/2012/04/30/no-one-inferior.

CHAPTER 6. The Activist's Attic

81 **only to be dismissed as insane** Some of the women who were deemed hysterical for objecting to their role in Victorian times were sent to psychologists, given electric shocks, or drained by leeches in the hope their "restlessness would abate"; in America, "angry" women were fitted with "scold's bridles," iron masks that both covered their faces and stilled their tongues.

86 **The sin . . . is challenging male authority** Sydney Anglican clergy wife Lesley Ramsey wrote in 1996: "Over the past thirty years of ministry in Anglican churches in Sydney, I have wrestled with God over my status as a woman. I don't know any woman who hasn't, because it is part of our rebellious nature." *Southern Cross,* winter 1996, 18.

87 **if such a woman approaches the pulpit** MOW *National Magazine,* April 1992, 6.

90 **"a large number of people became outraged"** Adam Hochschild, *Bury the Chains: The British Struggle to Abolish Slavery* (London: Pan Macmillan, 2012).

90 **One report estimated** Ibid.

93 **"Through archives, the past is controlled"** Joan M. Schwartz and Terry Cook, "Archives, Records, and Power: The Making of Modern History," *Archival Science* 2 (2002): 1–19. For an analysis of how this worked in the national archives of the apartheid regime in South Africa, see Verne Harris, "Redefining Archives in South Africa: Public Archives and Society in Transition, 1990–1996," *Archivaria,* fall 1996, 42; and "Claiming Less, Delivering More: A Critique of Positivist Formulations on Archives in South Africa," *Archivaria,* fall 1997, 44.

94   **"every protest shifts the world's balance"** Rebecca Solnit, "Every Protest Shifts the World's Balance," *The Guardian*, June 1, 2019.

CHAPTER 7. Honor the Temporary

96   **ephemera** Per WordReference.com.
99   **"Hope and peace have to include"** Anne Lamott, *Almost Everything: Notes on Hope* (New York: Riverhead Books, 2018), 132.

CHAPTER 8. Accept Imperfection

104   **"When you look at the clouds"** Alan Watts, *The Tao of Philosophy* (Clarendon, Vt.: Tuttle Publishing, 1999).
105   **she knew that she didn't look "fine"** Zadie Smith, *On Beauty* (London: Hamish Hamilton, 2005), 197–98.
108   **Diana Vreeland as having the "face of a gargoyle"** Daphne Merkin, "The Unfairest of Them All," *The New York Times*, October 16, 2005.
108   **Catherine the Great looked** Jonathan Jones, "Who Says David Cameron's No Oil Painting?," *The Guardian*, December 18, 2013.
108   **"He was not a pretty man"** Lecture by W. M. H. Herndoe, quoted in *The New York Times*, December 31, 1865.
109   **"the length and breadth of her dominions"** George Bernard Shaw, "The Ugliest Statues in London," *Arts Gazette*, May 31, 1919, 273; cited in Stanley Weintraub, "Exasperated Admiration: Bernard Shaw on Queen Victoria," *Victorian Poetry* 25, nos. 3/4 (autumn/winter 1987): 131.
110   **Plutarch wrote that her beauty** Plutarch, *Antony and Cleopatra*, from *Lives of Illustrious Men*, trans. John Dryden and Arthur Hugh Clough, bartleby.com/library/prose/4099.html.
110   **"They were always conscious"** From Elizabeth Jolley, *The Orchard Thieves* (New York: Viking, 1995).

111 **"Being thought of as a beautiful woman"** Carolyn Mahaney and Nicole Mahaney, *True Beauty* (Wheaton, Ill.: Crossway, 2014), 19.

112 **"like an aging female Dead Head with alopecia"** Meredith F. Small, "Mummy Reveals Egyptian Queen Was Fat, Balding and Bearded," *Live Science*, July 6, 2007.

112 **"an understated beauty"** Andrew Juniper, *Wabi Sabi: The Japanese Art of Impermanence* (Boston: Tuttle, 2003), 51.

113 **"We do prefer a pensive luster to a shallow brilliance"** Junichiro Tanizaki, *In Praise of Shadows*, trans. Thomas J. Harper and Edward G. Seidensticker (London: Vintage, 1991), 11–12.

115 **"busy and lively and unconcerned with self"** Spoken by the character Willy in Iris Murdoch's *The Nice and the Good* (New York: Random House, 2009), 179.

117 **"such a great example [in] how she carries herself"** Alexander Mallin, "Obama Says He's Not Worried About His Daughters Dating: 'They Have Secret Service,'" abcnews.go.com, November 4, 2016.

CHAPTER 9. Let Yourself Go

119 **"Girl! Girls are not to my taste"** See "The Meaning and Origin of the Expression: Mutton Dressed as Lamb," Phrase Finder, phrases.org.uk/meanings/mutton-dressed-as-lamb.html.

120 **"The worst thing you can do"** Cynthia Nellis with Kim Johnson Gross, "The Best Fashion Tips for Women Over 40," liveabout.com, January 10, 2018.

120 **women should "start dressing down"** Bianca London, "Carol Vorderman Dishes Out Style Advice for Older Women as It Is Revealed That Most Females Change Their Wardrobes When They Hit 50," *Daily Mail*, July 4, 2013.

120 **"a bob at this stage"** Shane Watson, "The 40 Things

Every Woman Should Know About Fashion Over 40," *The Telegraph*, September 4, 2018.

120 **"Are you a middle-aged fashionista?"** "Top 10 Items You're Too Old to Wear," *Everyday Health*, November 15, 2017.

120 **"The sulky, not bothered expression"** Watson, "40 Things Every Woman Should Know About Fashion."

121 **"It's about being adored, not ravaged"** Lisa Armstrong, "How to Dress Your Age for Spring 2015," *Harper's Bazaar*, April 2015.

123 **"We all get dressed for Bill"** Matthew Schneier, "Bill Cunningham Left Behind a Secret Memoir," *The New York Times*, March 21, 2018.

123 **"his delight in the possibility of you"** Hilton Als, "Bill Cunningham Was So Alive," *The New Yorker*, September 5, 2018.

PART III. Walking Each Other Home

135 **"We are all just walking"** Ram Dass and Mirabai Bush, *Walking Each Other Home: Conversations on Loving and Dying* (Boulder, Colo.: Sounds True, 2018).

136 **a book I had just given her** Hannah Kent, *Burial Rites* (London: Pan Macmillan, 2013).

CHAPTER 11. Freudenfreude: Sharing the Joy

139 **"Most women know, that as soon as their back is turned"** Rachael Oakes-Ash, *Anything She Can Do, I Can Do Better: The Truth About Female Competition* (Sydney: Random House, 2011).

145 **"Empathy works wonders"** Catherine Chambliss and Amy C. Hartl, eds., *Empathy Rules: Depression, Schadenfreude, and Freudenfreude: Research on Depression Risk Factors and Treatment* (New York: Nova Science Publishers, 2017), xiii–xiv.

145 **In 2016, Professor Chambliss replicated her findings**
Ibid.
146 **subjects who underwent Freudenfreude Enhancement
Training** Catherine Chambliss et al., "Reducing Depression via Brie Interpersonal Mutuality Training (IMT): A
Randomized Control Trial," *International Journal of
Health Sciences* 2, no. 1 (March 2014): 26.
146 **"[You cannot] say women aren't bitches"** Roxane Gay,
Bad Feminist: Essays (London: Constable & Robinson,
2014). Also excerpted in *The Guardian*, as "Roxane Gay:
The Bad Feminist Manifesto," August 2, 2014.

CHAPTER 12. She Trashed Her Golden Locks

149 **"When I was a girl"** Tim Winton, *Cloudstreet* (Ringwood,
Australia: Penguin, 1998), 231.
157 **"The first time a boy hurt me"** Anaïs Nin, *Ladders to Fire*
(New York: E. P. Dutton, 1946), 108.
157 **what Joan of Arc was burned at the stake for** It's true also
that when she began wearing male clothing again, after
promising not to, this amounted to repeat offending. As the
author of the novel *The Last Days of Jeanne d'Arc*, Ali
Alizadeh, explained to me, when asked by the judges why
she had done this, Joan said she had been told to by "her
Voices" and "since at her abjuration she had explicitly
(under much duress) denied that she had ever heard her
Voices, her saying now that she was (still) hearing them
amounted to an absolute recantation. It was then that this
recantation, at another trial session, was found to amount
to the crime of Relapse (i.e., lapsing backing into Heresy).
And the punishment for Relapse was death by fire."
157 **she wanted to dress like a man so she could act like a
man** As suggested by Ali Alizadeh in *The Last Days of
Jeanne d'Arc* (Sydney: Giramondo, 2017).
158 **The court notary testified that this had been the case**
This comes from the deposition on May 12, 1456, given by

Guillaume Manchon, who had been the chief notary at Joan of Arc's trial; cited in Robert Wirth, ed., "Primary Sources and Context Concerning Joan of Arc's Male Clothing," *Joan of Arc: Primary Sources Series* (St. Cloud, Minn.: Historical Association for Joan of Arc Studies, 2006), 5.

158 **"many times too, in sport, he tried to touch her breasts"** Juliet Barker, *Conquest* (Cambridge, Mass.: Harvard University Press, 2012), 148.

CHAPTER 13. Burning Bright: Candy Royalle

166 **Candy spoke of yearning to live** Candy Royalle, "Birthing the Sky, Birthing the Sea," from *A Trillion Awakenings* (Perth, Australia: UWA, 2018), used with permission.

167 **wrote about being a "bold, queer Arabic woman"** Candy Royalle, "Here, Queer and Arabic: On the Road to Belonging," Overland, May 11, 2016.

167 **"We utilize things like art and activism to create a place of belonging"** Ibid.

170 **"I felt very acutely that a sense of suffering"** Burke, "Rock Star Was Asked What God's Voice Sounds Like."

PART IV. Invincible Summer

173 **"In the midst of winter"** Albert Camus, "Retour to Tipasa," in *Summer (L'Été)* (Albert Camus, Œuvres complètes, cit., III, 1954), 613.

Regarde: *Look, and savor*

175 **"*Regarde*, little darling, the hairy caterpillar"** Colette, *Earthly Paradise: An Autobiography* (London: Secker & Warburg, 1966), 28.

175 **"Throughout my existence"** Judith Thurman, *A Life of*

Colette: Secrets of the Flesh (London: Bloomsbury, 2000), 497.

176 **"The sky was as heavy as a pot cover"** Thurman, *A Life of Colette*, 498.

CHAPTER 14. Thoughts for My Son: The Art of Savoring

179 **"I have discovered"** Paul Hiller, *Arvo Pärt* (Oxford: Oxford University Press, 1997), 87.

181 **a stubborn gladness** From Jack Gilbert's poem "A Brief for the Defense," where he writes, "We must have the stubbornness / to accept our gladness in the ruthless / furnace of this world."

182 **"like swishing the experience around"** Fred Bryant, *Savoring: A New Model of Positive Experience* (Philadelphia: Routledge, 2006).

185 **may unlock some of the biological mysteries** Aaron S. Heller et al., "The Neurodynamics of Affect in the Laboratory Predicts Persistence of Real-World Emotional Responses," *The Journal of Neuroscience* 35, no. 29 (July 2015): 10503–9.

185 **"The secret to happiness"** Barry Schwartz, "Are We Happier When We Have More Options?," *TED Radio Hour*, NPR, November 15, 2013.

185 **The Danes have long known this** Robb B. Rutledge et al., "A Computational and Neural Model of Momentary Subjective Well-Being," *PNAS* 111, no. 33 (August 2014): 12252–57.

186 **"If expectations are unrealistically high"** Kaare Christensen, Anne Maria Herskind, and James W. Vaupel, "Why Danes Are Smug: Comparative Study of Life Satisfaction in the European Union," *BMJ* 333 (2006): 1289.

186 **"Type A's focus on how proud they are"** Fred B. Bryant and Paul R. Yarnold, "Type A Behavior and Savoring Among College Undergraduates: Enjoy Achievements

Now—Not Later," *Optimal Data Analysis* 3 (April 4, 2014): 25–27. See also J. L. Smith and F. B. Bryant, "Are We Having Fun Yet?: Savoring, Type A Behavior, and Vacation Enjoyment," *International Journal of Wellbeing* 3, no. 1 (2012): 1–19.

187 **Asceticism . . . has benefits for happiness** Jordi Quoidbach and Elizabeth W. Dunn, "Give It Up: A Strategy for Combating Hedonic Adaptation," *Social Psychological and Personality Science* 4, no. 5 (January 2013): 1–6. In another study, by University of Michigan psychologist Ed O'Brien, fifty-two people were told they were participating in a taste test for Hershey's chocolate. They were told to draw five chocolates in several flavors—milk, dark, caramel, almond, crème—out of a bag, then rate each out of ten. Some of the group were told before taking out the fifth chocolate that it would be their last one. All of these people rated the last chocolate as the best, and the entire experience overall as more enjoyable. See Ed O'Brien and Phoebe C. Ellsworth, "Saving the Last for Best: A Positivity Bias for End Experiences," *Psychological Science* 23, no. 2 (2012): 163–65.

187 **"entitlement is a toxic narcissistic trait"** Case Western Reserve University, "Entitlement May Lead to Chronic Disappointment," *Science Daily*, September 13, 2016. For source document, see J. B. Grubbs and J. J. Exline, "Trait Entitlement: A Cognitive-Personality Source of Vulnerability to Psychological Distress," *Psychological Bulletin* 142, no. 11 (2016): 1204–26.

188 **rich people ate more quickly and enjoyed less** Jordi Quoidbach et al., "Money Giveth, Money Taketh Away: The Dual Effect of Wealth on Happiness," *Psychological Science* 21, no. 6 (2010): 759–63. As Quoidbach and Dunn have said, the relationship between wealth and happiness is "surprisingly weak."

188 **"experience stretching"** Daniel Gilbert, *Stumbling on Happiness* (New York: Knopf Doubleday, 2006).

188 "experiencing the best things in life" Quoidbach et al.,
     "Money Giveth, Money Taketh Away": 759–63. Quoid-
     bach claimed his 2010 study provided the first evidence
     that money impairs an ability to savor everyday experi-
     ences.
188 "one need not actually visit" Michel Pireu, "How Money
     Can Detract from the Simple Pleasures of Daily Life,"
     Business Day, July 23, 2010.

CHAPTER 15. Ert, or a Sense of Purpose

191 after hearing her talk on the radio *Conversations*, ABC
     Radio National, May 2, 2017.
192 "I don't think it needs to be jellyfish" Ibid.
195 Whatever propels you forward For millions, ert is spiritual
     practice. As Professor Vicki Grieves wrote, the beliefs and
     practices of the ancient Indigenous cultures of Australia
     can provide "community and connectedness with land and
     nature including proper nutrition and shelter." Illustrating
     yet again how much we have to learn from this ancient
     culture, Grieves, who is of Warrimay and Tasmanian de-
     scent, says it also entails "feeling good about oneself,
     proud of being an Aboriginal person. It is a state of being
     that includes knowledge, calmness, acceptance and toler-
     ance, balance and focus, inner strength, cleansing and
     inner peace, feeling whole." Vicky Grieves, "Aboriginal
     Spirituality: Aboriginal Philosophy—the Basis of Aborigi-
     nal Social and Emotional Wellbeing" (discussion paper
     no. 9, Cooperative Research Centre for Aboriginal Health,
     2009), 7.
195 "jewels as big as my seven-year-old hand" Michael
     McCarthy, *The Moth Snowstorm: Nature and Joy* (London:
     John Murray, 2016), 5.
196 "threatened every bone in my uninhibited body" Hilton
     Als, "Bill Cunningham Was So Alive," *The New Yorker*,
     September 5, 2018.

196 **"I just loved to see"** "Bill Cunningham on Bill Cunningham," *The New York Times*, June 25, 2016.
197 **"spiritual practice"** Als, "Bill Cunningham Was So Alive."
199 **"I go into my study and work"** Rachel Cooke, "Claire Tomalin: 'Writing Induces Melancholy. You're Alone, a Hermit,'" *The Guardian*, September 24, 2011.

CHAPTER 16. Growing by the Light of the Moon

200 **"The bud seemed to follow the moon"** Frank Crisp et al., eds., *Journal of the Royal Microscopical Society, Containing Its Transactions and Proceedings and a Summary of Current Researches Relating to Zoology and Botany (Principally Invertebrata and Cryptogamia), Microscopy, &c.* (London: Royal Microscopical Society, 1883), 2:534. See also Jacob Aron, "Moon's Gravity Could Govern Plant Movement Like the Tides," *New Scientist*, August 17, 2015; Peter W. Barlow, "Leaf Movements and Their Relationship with the Lunisolar Gravitational Force," *Annals of Botany* 116, no. 2 (August 2015): 149–87; Marissa Fessenden, "Plants Might Move with the Moon Just as the Oceans Do with the Tides," Smithsonian.com, August 19, 2015.
201 **"I don't have much knowledge"** Rainer Maria Rilke, *Selected Poems of Rainer Maria Rilke* (New York: Harper & Row, 1981), 55.
202 **Christianity, he said, "is almost solely based on suffering"** Elie Wiesel, "The Art of Fiction No. 79," *Paris Review*, no. 91 (spring 1984).
202 **"if there is a meaning in life at all"** Viktor E. Frankl, *Man's Search for Meaning* (New York: Pocket Books, 1984), 88.

CHAPTER 17. Lessons on Hope from the Hanoi Hilton

208 **"Variable, and therefore miserable"** John Donne, *The Complete Poetry and Selected Prose of John Donne*, ed. Charles M. Coffin (New York: Modern Library, 1952), 415.

208 **"What is to give light must endure burning"** Anton Wildgans, *Helldunkle Stunde* (*Helldark Hour*), written in 1916, and quoted by Viktor E. Frankl in *The Doctor and the Soul: From Psychotherapy to Logotherapy* (London: Souvenir Press, 2012), where it is translated as quoted in this book. The sentence is sometimes translated as "What should shine, must tolerate that it burns." Note also that this quote is often wrongly attributed to Frankl.

211 **"a man detached"** James Stockdale, "Courage Under Fire: Testing Epictetus's Doctrines in a Laboratory of Human Behavior," *Hoover Essays* no. 6 (1993): 6, Hoover Institution on War, Revolution and Peace, creativecommons.org/licenses/by-nd/3:0/.

211 **"Would you have someone else be sick"** Ibid., 7. Stockdale was quoting Epictetus in *Enchiridion*.

211 **watched his plane land in a rice paddy** "Admiral James B. Stockdale," Academy of Achievement, June 26, 2019.

211 **"After ejection I had about thirty seconds"** Stockdale, "Courage Under Fire," 7.

212 **"my opinions, my aims, my aversions"** Ibid.

212 **an "object of contempt," a criminal** Stockdale also wrote, "Make sure in your heart of hearts, in your inner self, that you treat your station in life with *indifference*, not with contempt, only with *indifference*." Ibid., 9.

212 **"thundering herd of men ran toward him"** "Admiral James B. Stockdale," Academy of Achievement.

214 **"the life was never the same"** Ibid.

214 **"I never lost faith in the end of the story"** Jim Collins, *Good to Great: Why Some Companies Make the Leap and Others Don't* (New York: HarperBusiness, 2001), 83–85.

215 **"Oh, they were the ones who said"** Ibid. Also quoted on Collins's website, at jimcollins.com/media_topics/ TheStockdaleParadox.html.

215 **"This is a very important lesson"** Ibid.

216 **"Be joyful even though"** Wendell Berry, "Manifesto: The Mad Farmer Liberation Front," in *The Mad Farmer Poems*, large print edition (Canada: ReadHowYouWant.com, Limited, 2010).

216 **"God talks in the trees"** Excerpt from Thomas Merton, *The Sign of Jonas* (New York: Harcourt, Brace, 1953).

CHAPTER 18. Raiding the Unspeakable

217 **"In his sleep, he holds up 'the wall' "** Joanne Kimberlin, "Our POWs: Locked Up for 6 Years, He Unlocked a Spirit Inside," *The Virginian-Pilot*, November 11, 2008.

218 **"The kingdom, Jesus taught . . . belongs to the poor"** Rachel Held Evans, *Inspired: Slaying Giants, Walking on Water, and Loving the Bible Again* (Nashville, Tenn.: Nelson Books, 2018), 153–54.

220 **spiritual practices like meditation and yoga** Art Raney, Daniel Cox, and Robert P. Jones, "Searching for Spirituality in the U.S.: A New Look at the Spiritual but Not Religious," Public Religion Research Institute, June 11, 2017, prri.org/research/religiosity-and-spirituality-in-america/.

221 **"The greatest attraction to investigating spirituality"** Mark McCrindle, *Faith and Belief in Australia: A National Study into Religion, Spirituality and Worldview Trends* (Sydney: McCrindle Research, 2017). The major repellent, or turnoff, for people walking into a church, was "hearing from public figures and celebrities who are examples of that faith." The study was conducted after years of protracted opposition to same-sex marriage in this country, in which many churches invested heavily, and during which horrendous things were said by prominent Chris-

tian politicians and leaders about gays and lesbians. It was as though there was only one message coming from the church.

222 **"We now all know"** "Anglican Bishop Enters Gay Marriage Debate," *Gippsland Times*, May 18, 2012.

223 **"He didn't patronize my people or me"** Minniecon was reluctant when McIntyre asked if he would work with the Anglican Church in Redfern decades ago, responding: "With the Crown as its head, the Anglican Church in Australia represented the dispossession and destruction of my people." But he trusted McIntyre, who "became our greatest advocate, supporter, and also our greatest protector."

226 **"The saved one was very keen to meet Tim"** Helen Garner, *Everywhere I Look* (Melbourne, Victoria: Text Publishing, 2016), 36–37.

228 **She was then working on her new book about sex** In *Shameless* (New York: Crown, 2019), she tells us to take antiquated ideas about sex and "burn them the fuck down." She looks at how conservative ideas about sexuality can screw with people's brains, and suggests women send her their purity rings so she and an artist friend can melt them and make them into a sculpture of a vagina. This did not win her universal acclaim. But when she left her Denver parish after ten years to become a public theologian, her congregation gave her a stole with an image of Wonder Woman on it.

229 **"I've never fully understood"** Nadia Bolz-Weber, *Accidental Saints: Finding God in All the Wrong People* (New York: Convergent, 2015), used with permission.

229 **"Never once did Jesus scan the room"** Nadia Bolz-Weber, *Pastrix: The Cranky, Beautiful Faith of a Sinner and Saint* (New York: Jericho Books, 2013), used with permission. When the much-loved writer Rachel Held Evans died unexpectedly at the age of thirty-seven, Bolz-Weber, a close friend, gave this benediction at her funeral:

Blessed are the agnostics.
Blessed are they who doubt.
Blessed are those who have nothing to offer.
Blessed are the preschoolers who cut in line at
   communion.
Blessed are the poor in spirit.
You are of heaven and Jesus blesses you.

Blessed are those whom no one else notices.
The kids who sit alone at middle school lunch tables.
The laundry guys at the hospital.
The sex workers and the night-shift street sweepers.
The closeted. The teens who have to figure out ways to
   hide the new cuts on their arms.
Blessed are the meek.
You are of heaven and Jesus blesses you.

Blessed are they who have loved enough to know what loss
   feels like.
Blessed are the mothers of the miscarried.
Blessed are they who can't fall apart because they have to
   keep it together for everyone else.
Blessed are those who "still aren't over it yet."
Blessed are those who mourn.
You are of heaven and Jesus blesses you.

230 **"a rowling mawl of choruses"** Tim Winton, *The Boy Behind the Curtain: Notes from an Australian Life* (London: Pan Macmillan, 2017).

232 **Germaine Greer dismissed the Bible** Quoted in Meredith Lake, *The Bible in Australia: A Cultural History* (Sydney: New South Publishing, 2018), 308.

232 **"I think what you have with Christianity"** Susanna Rustin, "What Is the Meaning of Christmas?," *The Guardian*, December 21, 2012.

CHAPTER 19. Embracing Doubt

234 **"the doubt of the century"** Gopi Chandra Kharel, "The
Doubt of the Century? 'I Doubt If There Is God,' Says
Church of England Head," *International Business Times,*
September 20, 2014.

234 **"Atheism is on the rise"** Richard Hartley-Parkinson, "Divine
Disintervention: Archbishop of Canterbury Admits His
Doubts About God's Existence," *Metro,* September 18, 2014.

236 **"no suffering greater"** Sally Fitzgerald, ed., *The Habit of
Being: Letters of Flannery O'Connor* (New York: Farrar,
Straus and Giroux, 1979), 353.

236 **"Please pray specially for me that I may not spoil His
work"** Brian Kolodiejchuk, ed., *Mother Teresa: Come Be
My Light: The Revealing Private Writings of the Nobel
Peace Prize Winner* (London: Rider, 2008), 149.

237 **"System of morals"** Benjamin Franklin, *The Private Corre-
spondence of Benjamin Franklin, Comprising a Series of Let-
ters on Miscellaneous, Literary, and Political Subjects,
Written Between the Years 1753 and 1790, Illustrating the
Memoirs of His Public and Private Life, and Developing the
Secret History of His Political Transactions and Negociations*
[sic], *Now First Published from the Originals,* ed. William
Temple Franklin (London: Henry Colburn, 1817), 278.

237 **"the stupid are cocksure"** Bertrand Russell, *The Philosophical Totems of Bertrand Russell* (UB Tech, 2018), ebook.

239 **"the work of building"** René Descartes, *The Meditations,
and Selections from the Principles of Philosophy, of Descartes,* ed. and trans. John Veitch (United Kingdom:
Sutherland & Knox, 1853), 17.

239 **"To have doubted one's own first principles"** Oliver
Wendell Holmes, Jr., "Ideals and Doubts," *Illinois Law Review* 10, no. 3 (1915).

240 **"follow knowledge like a sinking star"** Alfred, Lord Ten
nyson, "Ulysses," in *Tennyson,* ed. W. E. Williams (London: Penguin, London, 1986), 58.

CODA. Floating in the Bardo

243   **"The first, the wildest and the wisest thing I know"** Mary
      Oliver, "Low Tide," *Amicus Journal* 18, no. 4 (winter
      1997): 32–43.

244   **"The trivia of everyday life falls away"** *Conversations*,
      ABC Radio National, December 13, 2017.

246   **"If you break your neck"** Robert Fulghum, *Uh-Oh: Some
      Observations from Both Sides of the Refrigerator Door* (New
      York: Random House, 1993), 146.

247   **"wounds that glowed in the dark"** James Byrne, *"Pho-
      torhabdus luminescens*: The Angel's Glow," The Naked
      Scientists (thenakedscientists.com), February 25, 2011.

250   **"than a broken woman"** Hannah Gadsby, *Nanette*, Net-
      flix, 2018.

250   **"absolutely unmixed attention is prayer"** Simone Weil,
      Gravity and Grace (New York: Routledge, 2004), 117.

251   **"When tragedy or misfortune comes our way"** His Holi-
      ness the Dalai Lama, *Ethics for the New Millennium* (New
      York: Riverhead Books, 1999), 139.

252   **"the rarest and purest form of generosity"** Miklos Vetö,
      The Religious Metaphysics of Simone Weil (Albany: State
      University of New York Press, 1994), 45.

252   **"How can you not want to be out there among all this
      stuff?"** *Conversations*, ABC Radio National, November 23,
      2017.

252   **"Who made the world?"** From Mary Oliver, *House of
      Light* (Boston: Beacon Press, 1990).

254   **three-quarters of all sea creatures have "biolumines-
      cence capability"** Séverine Martini and Steven H. D.
      Haddock, "Quantification of Bioluminescence from the
      Surface to the Deep Sea Demonstrates Its Predominance
      as an Ecological Trait," *Scientific Reports* 7, no. 45750
      (2017).

PERMISSION CREDITS

Grateful acknowledgment is made to the following for permission to reprint previously published material:

Nadia Bolz-Weber: Benediction from the funeral of Rachel Held Evans by Nadia Bolz-Weber and brief quotes from the writings of Nadia Bolz-Weber. Reprinted by permission of the author.

Charlotte Sheedy Literary Agency, Inc.: "The Summer Day" from *House of Light* by Mary Oliver, published by Beacon Press, Boston. Copyright © 1990 by Mary Oliver, used herewith by permission of the Charlotte Sheedy Literary Agency, Inc.

Frances Collin, Literary Agent: Excerpt from *Silent Spring* by Rachel Carson, copyright © 1962 by Rachel L. Carson and copyright renewed 1990 by Roger Christie; excerpt from *Always, Rachel: The Letters of Rachel Carson and Dorothy Freeman*

1952–1964, copyright © 1995 by Roger Allen Christie; excerpt from *The Sense of Wonder* by Rachel Carson, copyright © 1956 by Rachel L. Carson. Reprinted by permission of Frances Collin, Trustee.

Miriam Rose Foundation: Miriam Rose's writings on Dadirri. Dadirri is a word from the Ngangikurungkurr language. Miriam Rose is an Elder from the Nauiyu community, Daly River, Northern Territory, miriamrosefoundation.org.au.

UWA Publishing, The University of Western Australia: Quotes from a performance by Candy Royalle at the Red Rattler, excerpts from the poem "Birthing the Sky, Birthing the Sea" by Candy Royalle, and writings from "Overland" by Candy Royalle. Reprinted by permission.

ABOUT THE AUTHOR

JULIA BAIRD is an award-winning journalist, broadcaster, and bestselling author. She is an op-ed contributor for *The New York Times*, a columnist for *The Sydney Morning Herald* and *The Age*, and a host of *The Drum* on ABC TV (Australia). Her writing has also appeared in *Newsweek*, *The Philadelphia Inquirer*, *The Guardian*, *The Washington Post*, *The Monthly*, and *Harper's Bazaar*. Holding a Ph.D. in history from the University of Sydney, Baird is a former fellow at the Shorenstein Center on Media, Politics and Public Policy at Harvard University, and for several years was the senior editor for *Newsweek*. Her first book, *Media Tarts*, was based on her history Ph.D. about the portrayal of female politicians. Her last book, a biography of Queen Victoria, was published in several countries to critical acclaim and was named one of the top ten books of 2016 by Janet Maslin of *The New York Times*. She lives by the sea in Australia with two kids and an outsize dog.